PERSONAL

BANKRUPTCY

WHAT EVERYONE NEEDS TO KNOW

By: Patrick D. McBurney, Jr.

*For the reverence and fear of God are basic to all wisdom.
Knowing God results in every other kind of understanding.*

Proverbs 9:10 – The Living Bible

*This book is dedicated to the reader, who is looking for a
map out of their perfect financial storm.*

ACKNOWLEDGEMENTS

I would like to thank my family, my dear friend Dr. Robert F. Hogg, Ph.D., for editing my manuscript. Sean McGrath who paved the way by showing me that writing a good book can and should be done, and my secretary Christine Hawley for helping me with the manuscript, and too many other tasks to mention.

Contents

PERSONAL BANKRUPTCY: "WHAT EVERYONE NEEDS TO KNOW"

For information, please contact:

Patrick D. McBurney, Jr., 6855 W. Clearwater Ave., Suite A103, Kennewick, WA 99336.
Tel: 509-374-9886; Fax: 509-374-1296.

Legal Disclaimer & Terms

This book does not constitute legal advice.

Patrick McBurney, Attorney at Law, has provided this content for educational purposes only. The information provided herein is not intended to be legal advice. Rather, this book is a tool to assist you with the process of obtaining competent legal counsel. Reading this book does not create an attorney-client relationship between the reader and Patrick McBurney, Attorney at Law.

Patrick McBurney, Attorney at Law, makes no warranty, express or implied, about the accuracy or reliability of information contained in this book. Times change, and laws change. While the author has endeavored to provide current information, the reader needs to understand that some of the information provided herein may be outdated or may become outdated as time passes.

If you believe that you need legal services, there is no substitute for the advice of a competent, experienced attorney. Furthermore, you should not act or rely on the contents of this book without seeking the advice of an attorney, just as you should not rely on advertisements, websites such as Wikipedia, and so forth when facing a serious legal problem. Most people wouldn't perform surgery on themselves, nor should you seek to deal with a legal problem on your own.

Like any lawyer, Patrick McBurney, Attorney at Law does not guarantee or warranty the outcome of any legal matter. Patrick McBurney, Attorney at Law, is a licensed attorney in the State of Washington and the State of North Dakota. You may contact Patrick McBurney at 6855 W. Clearwater Ave., Suite A103, Kennewick, WA 99336, phone: 509-374-8996, fax: 509-3741296, or through my website: www.PatrickMcburney.com

Foreword

My name is Patrick McBurney. I've been practicing law for over 25 years. For most of that time, I've been a consumer bankruptcy attorney. I've also been a public defender, a divorce lawyer, and when called for, a general practitioner. However, my favorite area of law practice is bankruptcy—and why is that? You can do a very good job in a divorce case, but in the end, you're still left with a broken family that's been scarred by the experience. In criminal matters, it's often the case that the attorney doesn't have an innocent client who needs to be freed but instead is working to manage and obtain the least-bad outcome for someone who is definitely going to jail—the only question is how much time that person will serve in jail. Bankruptcy is the only area of practice that is virtually guaranteed to produce a good outcome for the client. I help people get a financial fresh start, and sometimes I've been able to change people's lives for the better in dramatic ways.

I've decided to write this book because I've noticed over the past few years that consumers are having to battle disinformation and sometimes outright lies from creditors, collection agencies, and the media too. Many people are unaware of the power and the benefits they can receive by filing for bankruptcy. Bankruptcy isn't for everyone, and there may very well be alternatives to a bankruptcy filing. I'll discuss that too. This book will help you determine if bankruptcy is right for you.

No one ever really wants to file for bankruptcy, but there are times when bankruptcy can be a tremendous help and can create new opportunities, especially if you're confronted by a financial disaster resulting from a long-term or severe illness, a change of employment, a divorce, collections, or other types of financial crises. Bankruptcy may well be a solution in those situations. You don't always have control over what happens to you, but bankruptcy can allow you to chart a course out of the financial storm. This book will help guide you out of that financial storm. I'm going to talk about different types of financial problems and how they lead people to bankruptcy as well as the process of going through bankruptcy and how to go forward after bankruptcy—go forward with a fresh start.

By helping you learn more about the process, it's my hope that you can make an intelligent decision to deal with your financial crisis. At some point, you may decide that bankruptcy is what you need to do. Please feel free to call me and set up a consultation. I make no guarantees, but I do believe I can help. If you're caught in a financial storm and feeling overwhelmed, one phone call might well solve it all. Make an appointment. I look forward to hearing from you.

Sincerely,
Patrick D. McBurney Jr.
Attorney at Law

1. What You Need to Know to Start

So, you've found yourself with overwhelming financial problems. You may be thinking about bankruptcy as a way to make the pain of your situation go away, a way to get a fresh start. This book has been written to provide general guidance and helpful advice to assist you in making decisions about how to approach your financial problems. When you have more debts than assets and when you don't have the ability to pay those debts as they come due, this can make you feel completely overwhelmed by circumstance. If you're in this situation, your first question might be what can creditors do to you?

1.1. What can creditors do to you?

Before you analyze what a creditor is likely to do to collect a debt, you need to determine what kind of debt you owe. A secured debt is one for which collateral is pledged to insure payment. Collateral is real property or personal property, such as your house/land or vehicles or other things. If you have a mortgage, that's a secured debt. If you have a car loan, that's a secured debt. In those cases, the house or the car serves as "security for the loan." So, what can the creditor do here? The creditor may take your house or your car if you don't pay the debt.

An unsecured debt is one in which there is no property that will be taken if you don't pay. This is the most common kind of debt. It can be a debt on a credit card. It can be a bill from a doctor or dentist. It can be a fine or fee. It can be a personal loan from a friend. The most common kind of unsecured debts are credit card debts. With credit card debts, the lender does not have a car or house to take away from you. What most lenders do with unsecured debts such as these is call you, text you, and email you until they persuade you to pay. After some period, sometimes as short as 90 days or as long as six months, the original creditor will turn the debt over to a third-party collection agency. This collector will also contact you to persuade you to pay the debt. Eventually, the unsecured creditor will be forced to file a lawsuit in order to obtain a court judgment to continue trying to collect the debt. That judgment can act as a lien on any real estate you own; the judgment can be used to order you to appear in court for a supplemental proceeding. That's a court hearing where a creditor can ask you questions about where you work and where you bank as well as questions about your assets. With that kind of information, the creditor can and likely will attempt to garnish your wages or bank account.

Many times, clients have told me, "Mr. McBurney, I went to the bank and all my money was suddenly gone," or "I just got my paycheck, and somebody is taking 25% of it. I don't know how that happened." Normally, what has happened is that at some point the client incurred a debt, the client was unable to pay it, the debt was turned over to a collection agency, the collection agency filed a lawsuit, it then served my client with the lawsuit (i.e., someone personally delivered legal documents to the client or someone who lived with the client), and my client didn't respond to the lawsuit. The result is that the creditor obtained a default judgment and began garnishing your money. Although you might be feeling overwhelmed and even depressed when in debt, it's crucial to pay attention to any mail and any papers that are delivered to you. If you get served with a lawsuit, it's important to consult with an attorney right away. You need expert advice about how to respond.

People sometimes ask me if collection agencies every fake service of process in a lawsuit? Sometimes they do, but when I look up information about the case and ask my clients about having been served, I usually discover that they actually did know about the lawsuit: "Well, my neighbor got the papers," or "My daughter got the papers and didn't tell me about the case until it was too late." Even when I determine that there was a problem with service of process, there's still no point in going back to court to set aside the judgment/suit because the client owes the debt in the first place.

If you're going to file for bankruptcy, you need to know that while most debts are dischargeable—meaning that after the bankruptcy process you won't owe those debts—some debts aren't dischargeable. I'll talk more about the bankruptcy discharge later, but for now, an example of dischargeable debts are credit card debts; student loans are an example of debts that are not usually dischargeable (although they can be discharged under certain circumstances).[1]

---

[1] I'll say more about dischargeability in subsequent chapters. Let me note right now, however, that there are certain situations in which credit card debt can become non-dischargeable and also situations in which student loans can be discharged. Both situations involve lawsuits in bankruptcy court. These lawsuits are called adversary proceedings.

1.2. If you ignore creditors, will they go away?

Believe it or not, creditors sometimes do just go away. While I usually don't recommend this as a strategy, there are some circumstances in which simply letting sleeping dogs lie is indeed the best strategy. Some time ago, I had a man come to my office who wanted to file for bankruptcy. He was concerned because he had several fines and many debts that had not been paid. He was certain that he'd face garnishments once he returned to work. He had just gotten out of prison (having served about five years due to a felony conviction). Now that he was free, he was anxious to go back to work to start making money. I kept asking him about who it was he owed money to. He told me that he didn't know, but he was sure he had a number of hospital bills, criminal traffic fines, and a host of other unpaid debts. He was also concerned that the unpaid traffic fines were going to prevent him from having a driver's license.

Finally, after talking to him for about 45 minutes, I decided to check his credit report. He was surprised to discover that there were no debts on it. I then went to the Department of Licensing website to see if his license was suspended. It wasn't. All my client needed to do to get his driver's license was simply pay a reinstatement fee.

The question is why this was the case, especially when my client was sure that he owed money and had a suspended license. The statute of limitations is part of the answer.[2] For

---

[2] Statutes of limitations can be found in the Revised Code of Washington (RCW) in RCW § 4.16.

example, my client had gone to the hospital in 2007. The bill had been $5000.00 and was eventually turned over to a collection agency. To collect that medical bill, the collector would have six years to file a lawsuit (due to the statute of limitations). Let's assume the collection agency didn't wait to sue you but filed the case in 2007 and obtained a judgment for $5,000.00. That money would need to have been collected before 2018 (within ten years). As of 2018, the $5,000.00 would have become uncollectible unless the creditor went to court to have the judgment extended for another ten years. My client discovered that due to the age of his debts, most if not all of what he owed was uncollectible thanks to the statute of limitations. I was glad to be able to tell the man that he didn't need to file for bankruptcy after all.

1.3. What are your options for dealing with creditors?

The first option is simply to pay what you owe. Paying a debt before it's turned into a judgment is the best option. That may not be possible due to your financial circumstances, however. The next step is to contact a non-profit credit counselor. The credit counselor will look at your debts, assets, and income. The company will then attempt to negotiate with your creditors with the goal of reducing interest rates and setting up a repayment plan. However, this only works if all the creditors agree to repayment terms. The benefit of a debt management plan is that you avoid bankruptcy. Again, it only works if all the creditors agree to a repayment plan—if they don't, then bankruptcy may be the better option. A debt management company may also help you get a consolidation loan, which will combine all your debts into one loan with one monthly payment. One problem with consolidation loans is that they often require security. A very common example of such a loan is a second mortgage. Bankruptcy may be a better option, because it may enable you to get rid of your debt without increasing the amount you owe on your home, for example.

Debt settlement is also an option if you have a large amount of money to begin with. I had a client who had large debts but who also had 25,000.00 in cash. I negotiated settlements with several of his creditors. One collection agency for Citibank agreed to accept $2,500.00 to settle a $10,000.00 debt. Bank of America took 50 cents on the dollar. The man thus avoided bankruptcy. Most people can't do debt settlement, however, because it requires that you have the cash on hand. If you don't, then bankruptcy may well be the better option.

1.4. Why do we have bankruptcy?

In the ancient world, there was essentially no concept of bankruptcy: If you had debts and you were unable to pay them, you were sold into slavery. In the United States, we derive much of the foundation of our law from English common law. Prior to the American Revolution, it wasn't uncommon for those who couldn't pay their debts to be sent to debtor's prison for indefinite periods of time until the debt was paid. In the 1600s and 1700s, men and women were also put into indentured servitude (meaning contractually sold as a servant for a period of years) either as payment for passage to the Americas or in exchange for release from debtor's prison. In the late 1700s and early 1800s, Great Britain was locking up 10,000 people a year for debt. After the Revolution and the adoption of the American Constitution, there were substantial reforms which began to eliminate debtor's prisons in both the US and Britain.

Although the Constitution authorized Congress to develop uniform laws related to bankruptcy,[3] imprisonment for debt was still common until the 1830s. Various states were starting to outlaw the practice at the time, and Congress passed a new bankruptcy act in 1841. That began a process culminating in the Bankruptcy Act of 1898, which created the bankruptcy system as we now know it. The Act was substantially modified into the Bankruptcy Code of 1978, and the last major revision came in 2005 with the passage of the Bankruptcy Reform and Consumer Protection Act (BACPA).

Bankruptcy has evolved from a quasi-criminal phenomenon into a system designed to rehabilitate honest debtors and allow them to get a fresh start. The bankruptcy system is a necessary component of the economy. It allows people to take risks and pursue innovation and progress—people can try, fail, and start over once again.

Ultimately, the laws of the United States and Great Britain both developed from a strong Judeo-Christian tradition. According to the Biblical Book of Leviticus, there was a time for slaves and prisoners to be freed, debts to be forgiven, and the mercies of God to be made particularly manifest (see Leviticus 25:8-13). This was called Jubilee, and it's a founda-

---

[3]U.S. Constitution—Article I § 8—clause 4.

tional concept of bankruptcy law. The main point of is to allow people to continue to move forward with their economic lives, because if they can't, then society as a whole bears a more severe burden.

1.5. What do you do if you're afraid to answer the phone or go to the mail box?

Sometimes when you're under financial stress—even though debtor's prison has been outlawed—it still feels like someone might try to punish you because you can't pay your bills. On one occasion, I had a client who had no assets and whose only income was from Social Security. She shared with me that she felt such severe anxiety about these debts that she couldn't sleep. She told me that she got calls from people who were very rude and sometimes said that she was a bad person because she had debts. From a legal standpoint, however, she had nothing to worry about. I explained to her that the law doesn't allow collectors to garnish her bank account or take her Social Security. She couldn't be sued because her income (Social Security) was exempt, and she didn't have any assets. Although people can't be locked up these days just because they owe money, this woman had been living in a kind of debtor's prison in her mind. Bankruptcy allowed her to get a fresh start. She could now answer her phone and open her mail without feeling a heavy weight on her shoulders. She could now feel free again.

As we see from the example of this woman, debts can take a major toll on a person. I've had clients whose financial stress caused them to develop eating disorders, sleep disorders, marital difficulties, and generalized anxiety. You may feel trapped. It may seem that you're at the end of your rope. When I file bankruptcy for a client, I'm gratified that I can help lift their burdens and ease their distress.

1.6. What do you do if someone is suing you?

If you're being sued, you have a legal problem. It doesn't matter if you're being sued for negligence, divorce, or some other matter. While you can ignore some bad things and they may indeed go away, nine times out of ten ignoring a legal problem will make that problem worse. If you're served a summons and a complaint, you should immediately seek the advice of a competent attorney. You don't want to end up coming to my office and saying, "I don't understand—someone is garnishing my wages," or "They took all the money out of my bank account." Getting ahead of a situation means you should seek legal advice as soon as you're aware of a legal problem. Legal advice can help you avoid or at least manage unpleasant consequences in the future.

1.7. What do you do if someone is garnishing your wages?

If your wages are being garnished, bankruptcy will allow you to stop the garnishment and take control of your paycheck. If you can file bankruptcy soon enough, you may be able to stop the garnishment before it starts. Sometimes even after the wages have been garnished, it's possible to get them returned to you.

1.8. How long does the bankruptcy process take?

For most people, there are two possible types of bankruptcy, Chapter 7 and Chapter 13. I'll talk more about these later. However, typical Chapter 7 cases take about four months from the time the bankruptcy is filed to the time the client receives a discharge of debt. Chapter 13 cases involve a payment plan, which has a minimum term of 36 months and a maximum of 60 months. Your bankruptcy case can thus take as long as five years or as little as four months.

Depending upon the information you provide to my office, it's possible to have your bankruptcy filed in as little as three to four hours, although most bankruptcies take a couple of weeks to prepare, draft, review, and file.

1.9. How much does bankruptcy cost?

Bankruptcies can sometimes take months before they are filed. This is simply because the client needs time to gather the monies to pay the attorney's fees. Typically, the attorney's fees must be paid before the petition can be filed. Why? If your attorney doesn't collect all the fees upfront, the unpaid fees can be included and discharged in the bankruptcy. I usually tell clients that my wife becomes quite unreasonable when my attorney's fees get discharged.

According to Debt.org, the average bankruptcy attorney fees were between $1,500.00 and $4000.00 as of January of 2018. There are several factors that go into determining the cost of any bankruptcy: how many debts, the types of debts, whether there's a potential for an adversary lawsuit and whether there are any business assets involved. Everyone's case is different, so an attorney may charge more or less depending on the complexity of the case.

Chapter 7 bankruptcies have a filing fee of $335.00 (current as of January of 2018). This fee is usually paid to the attorney along with the attorney's fee to expedite filing (the filing fee for Chapter 13 bankruptcy is $310.00). If you have trouble coming up with the whole fee at the time of filing, you can request that the court allow you to pay it in three monthly installments. Just don't miss a payment because your case would then be dismissed.

Finally, there is the cost for credit counseling. By law, you need to have taken a credit counseling course prior to filing for bankruptcy. The cost of this service varies as well but typically ranges between $15.00 and $50.00 for individuals and couples. After filing for bankruptcy, you're also required by law to compete a debtor education course that also costs between $10.00 and $50.00 per couple.

2. What You Need to Know about Reasons People File for Bankruptcy

There isn't an easy answer to this question. The reasons people files for bankruptcy are unique to them. That being said, however, there are certain circumstances that seem to come up often. Among them are medical debt, divorce, other unanticipated changes in personal circumstances, overuse of personal credit, and business failure.

Bankruptcy has changed significantly since 2005 when Congress passed the Bankruptcy Reform and Consumer Protection Act (BRCPA). Since then, the country has endured a financial crisis, a recession, and a jobless recovery. Because of these events, banks have changed how they extend credit. Credit is not as freely available to ordinary people as it was prior to 2008, and Congress has made the process of filing for bankruptcy much more difficult. As a result, the number of bankruptcies filed from 2005 through 2017 has decreased every year.

2.1. How does medical debt cause bankruptcy?

While there have been fewer bankruptcy filings in recent years, an increasing percentage of filings relate to medical issues. This is usually the result of a traumatic medical event—such as a heart attack, cancer, or other serious illness—for which a person was either uninsured or underinsured. I know about this from personal experience. In 2013, I spent Thanksgiving Day in a local emergency room (ER) with my wife. She is a nurse and had collapsed at work. Her symptoms were unusual enough that she agreed to go to the ER, but only after friends had urged her to seek treatment (by the way, medical professionals often make the worst patients because of what they know). We spent most of the day before and then most of Thanksgiving Day itself in the ER. We saw three different doctors who called for a series of tests including blood work, a CAT scan, and an MRI. The results were inconclusive. While we were pleased to find out that there wasn't anything seriously wrong with my wife, the ER visit came at great cost. Because of changes in my wife's job situation, we were without insurance at the time. As a result, I received a $17,000 bill from the hospital. Using my skills as an attorney, I was ultimately able to reduce that bill to about $9,000.

This is an example of the kind of crisis that many people have faced. A sudden illness, a visit to the ER, maybe an admission to the hospital, emergency surgery, and suddenly you have $100,000 or $200,000 in medical bills, some of which may be covered by insurance and some of which may not. In this instance, even if your insurance covers 80% of the cost, you may still find yourself owing tens of thousands of dollars. The clients that I represent don't necessarily have the additional resources or the skill set that I had when I was uninsured, so even a $17,000 medical bill can create a perfect financial storm.

2.2. How does divorce cause bankruptcy?

Among the most tragic things I've observed in 25 years of practice as an attorney are all the wounds, all the collateral damage, caused by the dissolution of a marriage. I've seen people treat each other abominably during their breakups. Moreover, it's almost always the case that divorce doesn't leave people better off at all.

If some evening you come home only to discover your recliner, your LP & DVD collection, your bowling trophy, and other treasures sitting in your driveway, this could be a sign that you'll be encountering a perfect financial storm. If your key no longer works in the lock and you receive a "Dear John/Jane" letter, your world has now been turned upside down. After the shock of the separation, you may find that a judge will order you to pay new obligations, such as spousal support or child support. The court may also order you to pay certain debts, or you may find yourself left with all the bills when the other spouse isn't contributing (despite a court order requiring that). It's a perfect financial storm.

Before a divorce, the parties often had two incomes supporting one household. With each of those incomes now supporting a separate household, there'll be a significant decrease in the standard of living for everyone involved. Also, if the couple had been living paycheck to paycheck before, then each party may now need to make up the difference by borrowing from savings or by over-using credit cards. The parties may see a significant increase in personal, and a loss of assets may occur, such as repossessions of vehicles or a home foreclosure. This happens because there is simply not enough money to service all the debts.

I've seen divorce cases that are resolved amicably in 90 days and others that are fought tooth and nail for two or three years until brought to trial. In one instance, the parties continued to litigate the case for 10 years following their divorce trial. Most people will have a number of financial obligations stemming from their divorce such as attorney's fees and other new debts, such as child support. At the same time, many divorced people have fewer resources to meet those new obligations.

In divorce cases, it's typical to find that couples were financially overextended and in crisis long before deciding to end the marriage. Rather than dividing their debts in divorce court, the parties can sometimes resolve those issues by filing jointly for bankruptcy before filing for divorce. When couples have a lot of debt with few assets, bankruptcy can be a way to streamline the divorce process. If a divorcing couple files for bankruptcy before or during their divorce, they can rid themselves of most of their debt and walk out of the divorce court with a fresh start.

2.3. How do other unanticipated changes in personal circumstances cause bankruptcy?

Most people don't plan for tragedies such death, divorce, or serious illness, nor do most people anticipate being sued or charged with a crime. These things happen to the honest and the dishonest alike. In over 25 years of law practice, I've represented thousands of people in bankruptcies and hundreds of people in divorces. I've also had my share of criminal cases. On occasion, I've had the privilege of representing truly innocent people. Many of the people I've represented were indeed guilty, however, and my job in those cases was to obtain the best (or least-bad) possible outcome. In other words, it wasn't a question of whether the client was going to jail, but for how long and whether his or her criminal record would reflect a misdemeanor or a felony. In one of my bankruptcy cases, I represented a man who had gone to prison for five years for drug-related offenses. He had also been trying to run a business and had accumulated several debts. When he got out of prison, he wanted a fresh start. Though some of the debt wasn't collectible, there were civil judgments against him that made bankruptcy a good option for him.

A recent magazine article highlighted the fact that 47% of Americans don't have the ability to pay for a $400 emergency.[4] If that's the case with you, what happens when your car stops running? How can you deal with a broken furnace? What do you do when a natural disaster strikes? How do you face the loss of your job? Again and again, I've met debtors who got behind the eight ball due to crises like these. In many instances, they had no alternative but to file for bankruptcy to set things right again.

Bankruptcy can be used for more than just relief from the obligation to pay debt. Bankruptcy can also be used to reorganize your financial affairs and, in some cases, impose a plan of repayment of debt. Recently, I had a client who had been out of work for six months and had fallen behind on his mortgage. We filed a Chapter 13 bankruptcy for him to impose a plan of reorganization on the mortgage company. This client was able to use bankruptcy to save his home after he'd run out of other options. I'll talk more about Chapter 13

---

[4] Gabler, Neal, "The Secret Shame of Middle-Class Americans," *The Atlantic Magazine*, May 2016.

down the road, but it's important to mention it when discussing unforeseen circumstances.

2.4. How does overuse of personal credit lead to bankruptcy?

When I was first in practice as a bankruptcy attorney over 25 years ago, the most common reason my clients were filing for bankruptcy was the free availability of consumer credit. I especially remember the case of an elderly woman. She had over 20 credit cards with balances ranging from $1500 to $3000. Her sole source of income was Social Security. She received only about $800 per month and had to spend some $300 of that on prescription medications. She'd been paying for her prescriptions by using credit cards. She continued to get more offers for credit cards in the mail, and she would shift the balances from one card to another. I'll never forget this client. She was in my office crying and said, "I had such good credit." What struck me was the fact that this woman had made every minimum payment, but due her limited income, she had long passed the point of being able to repay her debts. The lesson I learned that day was that your worth as a person isn't determined by your credit score. I had a long talk with this woman, who was feeling a great deal of shame in having to file for bankruptcy. I told her that credit is merely a measurement used by financial institutions to determine if they're going to loan you money. A bad credit score doesn't mean that you're a bad person, nor does a good credit score mean that you're a good person. It's simply a factor that an institution uses to make business decisions.

There are plenty of bad people in this world and some of those bad people have excellent credit. There are a lot of good people in this world who have bad credit for weighty reasons such as serious illness, job loss, divorce, or other misfortunes. I refer to these people as "honest debtors." If your circumstances indicate that bankruptcy is likely to be in your future, you need to shift your perspective and look at your problem from a different perspective. While feeling guilt or shame may be natural in the circumstances, I want to tell you that it's okay to not feel guilt or shame. What I want you to feel once you understand your situation, once you have developed a plan (be it bankruptcy, credit counseling, or some other form of debt relief), is hope—hope because if you're an honest debtor, you'll be able to get relief from your debts and other financial obligations. You'll get a fresh start.

One of the other things I've observed in many years of bankruptcy practice is that it's important to develop good financial habits and discipline. These can be as simple as avoiding debt, keeping track of your money (e.g., balancing your checkbook every month), and keeping your expenses within your means. Credit cards are often overused for impulse purchases, such as automobiles. Before I started my law practice, I sold cars. Even though that was many years ago, I still draw on the lessons of that valuable experience. Automobiles are a big part of bankruptcy—trying to keep them, trying to get rid of them, and dealing with the aftermath of having them repossessed.

I've had several clients who went into a car dealership and simply spent more than they could afford because they wanted a certain type of vehicle. One client justified the purchase of a $60,000 car because of its exciting features and luxurious appointments. She felt that she simply needed that car. However, the need in question also came with a $900.00 per month payment. It was one reason (among others) that caused her to file bankruptcy.

In another case, my client was a husband getting a divorce. His wife had one of the vehicles, and for some reason, she had stopped making payments on it. It was eventually repossessed and then sold at auction for far less than what was owed on it. By the way, this is typical when vehicles are repossessed: After the bank gets the car back, it sells the vehicle at auction—usually for thousands of dollars (and sometimes tens of thousands of dollars) less than the amount of the loan. This left my client with what we call a repossession arrearage, and, as I recall, that amount was approximately $14,000. Because of this repossession debt, along with several credit card debts and a new child support obligation, bankruptcy helped the man start over and adjust to his new circumstances.

Automobile loans are probably the most common type of debt. Clients in bankruptcy cases want to do one of three things with these loans: first, reaffirm the loan (to keep the loan agreement and thus the vehicle; I'll discuss reaffirmation in more detail later); second, surrender the vehicle and/or discharge the repossession arrearage or third, use the bankruptcy process to adjust the payment and pay only the value of the vehicle. That third option is available in Chapter 7 through the process called redemption and in Chapter 13 as part of something called a "cramdown." Later, I'll discuss these and other terms.

Our bankruptcy laws are found in Title 11 of the United States Code, which is the body of law passed by Congress. Since the 19th century, there has been a process for discharging debts, that is, to excuse individuals and business entities from their legal responsibility to repay. While that might seem to be the same thing as canceling or erasing a debt, there is an important distinction. The order of discharge from the bankruptcy court excuses you from repayment. It doesn't erase the debts that you incurred; those debts remain and may still be on your credit report, even though you don't need to pay them.

Bankruptcy has evolved over time. Its purpose originally was to deal with businesses and to facilitate commerce. In fact, the entire Bankruptcy Code is written with businesses in mind. Even though most bankruptcy filings involve individual consumer debtors rather than businesses these days, it's still the case that facilitating business and commerce remains an important focus of the Bankruptcy Code.

My favorite business client was one I had a few years ago. This client had a dream—a dream of owning and operating his own business. For many years, he had been a pipefitter working a good union job at an excellent wage. He had access to credit and used several credit cards to finance the construction of a donut shop. He built a fine donut shop, doing about half the construction work himself. He opened the business and operated for about six months. Eventually, my client discovered something very important about himself— he was a bad donut maker. He simply couldn't make a profit.

However, he had over $100,000 of debt, not including the debt on his house and car. In his case, bankruptcy provided a path forward.

Every bankruptcy case that is filed is assigned a trustee. The trustee's purpose is to find property for what is known as the bankruptcy estate and sell that property for the benefit of creditors. Most of the time in Chapter 7 bankruptcy cases (the most common form of bankruptcy), people don't have any assets that the trustee is legally required to sell in order to pay off their debts. Clients usually ask me at our first meeting, "Can I keep my car?" or "Can I keep my house?" The good news is that the answer to both of those questions is usually yes thanks to bankruptcy law.

Getting back to the owner of the donut shop, the bankruptcy trustee in his case was presented with a turn-key donut business. So how was the case resolved? The bankruptcy trustee took over the donut shop, hired a realtor, and sold it as a complete business: countertops, refrigerators, deep fat fryers, mixers, and more. A very nice young couple bought the business for $35,000—tens of thousands of dollars less than what my client had spent to open the shop. After the trustee received that $35,000, some $10,000 went back to my client. Why? Because the law provides exemptions for tools of the trade and other business equipment (a competent attorney will help you find those kinds of exemptions). This left about $25,000 to pay back $100,000 worth of debt. Let's say, for example, that Citibank was owed $10,000. Here, Citibank received $.25 on the dollar and got paid $2500. This is how the bankruptcy laws are written and how bankruptcy is supposed to work. However, over 95% of debtors who file for bankruptcy don't have a spare donut shop—or an airplane or a beach house. Those people are called no-asset debtors (or no-asset filers). If you're a prospective bankruptcy debtor (and you don't own a donut shop), you're most likely a no-asset filer.

In another case, I represented a man who was a real entrepreneur. He'd presented a plan to the Washington State Department of Natural Resources and the United States Small Business Administration (SBA) for a process that he'd developed to reuse wood waste products to make specialized pellets for barbecues. My client believed in his invention, and so did the government because it gave him loan guarantees that resulted in commercial loans to start this business. My client's problem was that even though he'd developed a product and spent thousands of hours promoting it at trade shows, he wasn't able to create a large enough market to sustain production and sale of the product. My client had guaranteed his retirement accounts and personal real estate to the SBA in exchange for the loan guarantees. He had also incurred unpaid salaries and rents as well as other obligations above and beyond what he had guaranteed to the banks. Bankruptcy was necessary to close down this business and allow my client to move on with his life.

2.6. How will bankruptcy help stop your feelings of being overwhelmed?

When I meet prospective clients for the first time, the question I ask them is this: "What is the one thing that is causing you to come to my office and see me today?" Maybe it's one of the five examples discussed in this chapter (e.g., medical debt, divorce, other unanticipated changes in personal circumstances, overuse of personal credit, or business failure). Maybe it's a combination of factors, or maybe it's something else altogether. The bottom line is that no matter what caused the perfect financial storm, there's a way out.

When people hire me to represent them, they usually don't really know or understand what I can do for them. For most clients, filing bankruptcy is a bit of a leap of faith into the great unknown. Most clients have only a vague sense that bankruptcy might be a way out of the financial storm, which is what prompted them to call me in the first place.

Their sense is correct—bankruptcy is a powerful tool, a powerful remedy. When it's used correctly, it can stop foreclosures, garnishments, and lawsuits. It can get a repossessed vehicle returned to its owner. It can be used to restructure and impose a plan of repayment upon creditors. What it does best is relieve you, the honest debtor, of the legal responsibility to pay the debts you had prior to filing for bankruptcy. This is what it means to discharge a debt and what takes to get a fresh start.

3. What You Need to Know about the Process

An attorney who's represented thousands of people in bankruptcy needs to remind himself that each client is going through this process for the very first time. Therefore, it's vital to draw a clear map for clients. If you were a pioneer in the 1800s, you might have hired a guide to get you from St. Louis to the Oregon Territory. I think this analogy applies to bankruptcy. Your attorney is going to be your guide, and this section of the book is like a map showing you the starting point, the route, and the destination.

3.1. What is pre-bankruptcy credit counseling, and why do you need it?

Since the passage of the Bankruptcy Reform and Consumer Protection Act in 2005, credit counseling is required before a bankruptcy petition can be filed. Your attorney can recommend an approved credit counseling agency. Credit counseling takes about one hour. It can be done online or over the phone. The purported purpose of bankruptcy credit counseling is to make sure that debtors are aware of their options, including an appropriate debt management program.

In actuality, bankruptcy credit counseling is a speedbump put in place by Congress. It raises the cost of bankruptcy and makes filing more inconvenient. However, you should know that the credit counseling must be completed if you're planning to file a bankruptcy petition. You should also know that once you get a credit counseling certificate, it's only valid for

180 days. If you wait too long to file for bankruptcy, you'll have to retake the course.

3.2. What is a bankruptcy petition and why is it important?

Without the bankruptcy petition, there is no bankruptcy. The bankruptcy petition is the essential document that starts and guides the process of your bankruptcy. In most cases, what you're paying for when you hire an attorney is his expertise in preparing the bankruptcy petition correctly. It's a very complex document.

When I discuss this idea with clients, I often mention tax returns by analogy. Some people's tax returns are more complicated than others. The simplest situation is when you work for the same employer all year and have one W-2 form. However, if you're a self-employed small business owner, a managing agent of an LLC, or you have royalties and rental income, your tax return will be more complicated. The first two pages of your tax return are Form 1040, and attached to that are schedules, such as the earned-income tax credit schedule and the self-employment tax schedule.

A bankruptcy petition is usually a 50- to 80-page document consisting of six parts: the petition form itself, the schedules, the statement of financial affairs, the statement of intention, the means test, and the creditor matrix.

The petition portion of the "bankruptcy petition" is the part of the document that is like your tax return minus all the attachments. The petition section identifies you and states the type of bankruptcy you're filing (i.e., Chapter 7 or Chapter 13). It also provides the court with other relevant information about your case (e.g., Do you rent or own? Have you filed for bankruptcy before? Are you a business or consumer debtor?). Also, like your tax return, this form requires your signature. Quite literally this form is "you" asking the court for permission to file this case. In fact, filing these first five pages with the court is all that is required to start your bankruptcy case. However, it's necessary that all the other documents also get filed with the court in due course. If not, your case will be dismissed.

The next section of the bankruptcy petition contains the schedules, running from A through J. Schedule A is the real property schedule. If you own any real estate, you'd indicate its location and value on schedule A. Schedule B describes personal property. This is where we list your cash, furniture, vehicles, computers, business interests, debts that people owe you, and potential lawsuits if you may be entitled to recover damages. Schedule C is the exemption schedule. Exemptions can save your possessions from being sold off to pay your creditors. I'll discuss the crucial topic of exemptions below.

Schedules D, E, and F are what I call the debt schedules. Remember that a secured debt is one that has collateral. Your house and your car are examples, but other things can also be secured (e.g., boats, RVs, construction equipment, etc.). An unsecured debt doesn't have property attached to it that would be taken away from you in the event you fail to pay. Schedule D is where secured debts are listed.

Schedule E lists debts that are entitled to priority. Priority means that these debts get paid first if there's money in the bankruptcy estate. Money comes into the bankruptcy either through the sale of assets or through the funding of a Chapter 13 plan. Once there is money in your bankruptcy, creditors are notified, and they file claims to receive money from the bankruptcy court. The most common types of priority debts that a consumer bankruptcy debtor will have are taxes or child support/domestic support obligations. Another type of priority debt are the wages owed to employees.[5] These types of debts don't get discharged in bankruptcy.

Schedule F is a list of your other debts that aren't secured and aren't entitled to priority. In most cases, these debts are credit card bills, medical bills, personal loans, and other types of credit. It's usually the case that all these debts are dischargeable in bankruptcy, with one regular exception—student loans. Due to the 1998 amendments to the Higher Education Act, student loans are non-dischargeable in bankruptcy. However, there may be a way to address student loans in bankruptcy, through a bankruptcy lawsuit called an adversary proceeding.

Schedule H is where we list executory contracts. Examples include a lease on a car or an apartment. If you have a lease and you want to keep it, then you must assume the lease (i.e., this means that you're going to keep the lease and pay according to the terms of the lease agreement). If you don't assume the lease, it'll be rejected in your bankruptcy.

---

[5] The complete list of debts entitled to priority can be found under 11 U.S.C. § 507.

In order to make sure the lease isn't rejected because of the bankruptcy, you'll want to file a motion to have the bankruptcy court issue an order permitting the assumption of the leases you want to keep. This will allow you to keep your car or apartment.

Another example of an executory contract is an employment contract. When I was a public defender, I was an independent contractor. I had a contract with Benton County, WA, to provide public defense services for three years. I was paid a sum of money every month to handle a certain number of cases. If I failed to provide these services, I could be subject to penalties. In this example, the contract required me to provide services for a period of up to 90 days following the end of the contract. If I had filed for bankruptcy, I could have either filed a motion to assume the contract (thus keeping the remainder of the three-year contract in force), or I could have gotten out of my employment contract. Executory contacts or leases are usually financial burdens. More often than not, it's in the interest of a client to reject them rather than assume them.

Schedule G is where we list co-debtors. If you're filing bankruptcy with your spouse, then your spouse would not be listed as a co-debtor. Why? This is because your spouse is filing bankruptcy with you jointly. If you're filing for bankruptcy and your spouse isn't filing, then you'd list your spouse as a co-debtor. The question is then a co-debtor to which debts? Not every debt that you incur is the responsibility of your spouse. In most states, you must have a contractual relationship with the lender to be liable for a debt. This means, for example, that credit cards in your name but not your spouse's name are solely your responsibility. Conversely, credit cards only in her name are solely her responsibility. If both your names are on the credit card account, then it's a joint responsibility. If your spouse isn't filing, then she'd be listed as a co-debtor for your joint debt.

Take note regarding the community-property states: Arizona, California, Idaho, Louisiana, Nevada, New Mexico, Texas, Washington, and Wisconsin. If you live in a community-property state, you may be liable for debts of the marital community (i.e., your spouse's debts), even if the debt in question is only in your spouse's name.

Quite often, people co-sign a loan for a relative: For example, Uncle Bob is persuaded by his niece Brandy to help her get a car or another extension of credit. Bob co-signs for the loan and thus becomes a co-debtor. Typically, I hear from Uncle Bob when Brandy stops making the payments. At that point, Bob either has to make the payments himself or consider the possibility of bankruptcy if he's unable to pay. If Brandy files for bankruptcy, I'd list Uncle Bob as a co-debtor on Schedule G. My advice is that you should avoid being a co-debtor whenever possible, unless you're prepared to pay the full amount of the debt.

Schedule I is the income schedule. This is where you list your income from all sources and calculate just how much net income you have available for payments per month. Schedule J is where you list your expenses. On Schedule J, your expenses are subtracted from your income. Typically, that amount is very low or a negative number.

Finally, after schedules A thru J, there is a declaration that you sign under penalty of perjury stating that the information in the schedules is true and correct.

3.3. What is a 341 meeting of creditors? Does this mean we're going to court?

Due process of law is a phrase that you've heard before but most likely don't understand. It's a simple concept. What it means is <u>notice and opportunity to be heard</u>. When the government is going to alter your rights, you're entitled to due process. In the bankruptcy context, it's primarily the due process rights of creditors that we're concerned with. By filing bankruptcy, you're altering their rights to collect debts, and they're entitled to notice and an opportunity to be heard on the issue.

Hence, creditors receive notice of the bankruptcy and have a couple of opportunities to participate. First, there's the 341 meeting, also called a meeting of creditors (the part of the Bankruptcy Code that requires this meeting is section 341).[6] Is this a court hearing? Yes and no. it's not a traditional court hearing like you see on *Perry Mason* or *The People's Court* or *Judge Judy*. The bankruptcy judge doesn't participate at this hearing. Instead, the hearing is conducted by the bankruptcy trustee. The bankruptcy trustee is a special representative appointed by the Department of Justice whose job is to sell property for the benefit of creditors. Usually, the meeting of creditors occurs at a federal building, but I've at-

---

[6] See 11 U.S.C. § 341.

tended such meetings in hotel conference rooms, community centers, grange halls, at the Public Utility District auditorium, and other locations where space can be found. This hearing is on the record, which means that you're under oath and your statements are subject to penalty of perjury. If you intentionally lie at this meeting, you can be subject to civil and criminal penalties.

The purpose of this meeting is to give creditors and the bankruptcy trustee an opportunity to ask you questions about your case. The trustee asks questions because he's trying to find assets that could be sold to provide money for the benefit of the creditors you've listed in your bankruptcy petition. Remember the donut shop example—that business was sold, and some of the proceeds were available to distribute to creditors. Occasionally, creditors will show up at these meetings, but that's rare. When they do appear, the trustee will give them an opportunity to ask questions. The following is an example of questions and answers at a typical 341 meeting:

Trustee: Please raise your right hand. Do you swear to tell the truth, the whole truth, and nothing but the truth, so help you God?

Client(s): I do.

Trustee: Do you have identification?

Client(s): [At this point the trustee is provided with picture ID, and either a Social Security card or a document with your Social Security number on it].

Trustee: I'm looking at the driver's license of the debtor, and it's consistent with the information contained in this petition. I'm looking at the Social Security card of the debtor and the joint debtor, and these are also consistent with the information contained on the petition. Mr. & Mrs. Smith, this meeting is being recorded, and you're under oath.

Trustee: Are you Mr. and Mrs. Smith?

Client(s): Yes.

Trustee: Do you live at 1234 Main St., Anywhere, Washington 98111.

Client(s): Yes.

Trustee: Other than the house at 1234 Main St., have you owned any other real estate in, say, the last five years?

Client(s): No. [if the answer is yes, that information is most likely contained in the bankruptcy petition, and there may be a discussion as to the value and disposition of that property.]

Trustee: Mr. and Mrs. Smith, I've looked at your bankruptcy schedules, and I see that your home is worth $150,000. How did you come up with this valuation?

Client(s): [There are several possible answers to this question, but we'll use the most common one:] My attorney went to the tax assessor's website and looked up the tax assessed value, and that's the value we're using.

Trustee: All right. Question: Have you been in an accident, suffered an injury, or are you suing someone and, if so, do you expect to recover money?

Client(s): No. [If the answer is yes, you need to know that the bankruptcy trustee will most likely ask you for more detailed information about the lawsuit. The trustee will be very interested in lawsuits due to the potential for the bankruptcy estate to get money from the suit to pay your creditors.]

Trustee: Do you expect that in the next six months, someone will die and leave you a large sum of money?

Client(s): No. [If you do receive an inheritance within six months of filing for bankruptcy, that will be a source of funds to repay creditors.]

Trustee: Are there any creditors here who wish to examine Mr. and Mrs. Smith? Hearing none, that will conclude your meeting.

The dialogue above provides an example of the questions typically asked at a 341 meeting. Most of the time, creditors don't appear to ask questions. I've seen creditors appear in several circumstances. One type of situation involves local creditors such as a bank, furniture store, or tire store. The creditor may either try to persuade you to sign a reaffirmation agreement (an agreement where you and that creditor agree that bankruptcy didn't happen between you and that creditor), or the creditor will try to make arrangements with you to return the property that secures the loan. This is not a high-stress situation. It's often an opportunity to have credit extended after bankruptcy or, alternatively, resolve the issue about what to do with a car or personal property such as tires, refrigerators, washers and dryers, and so forth that are secured by a purchase money security interest.[7]

Here's a second situation in which representatives of a creditor did show up at a 341 meeting. A well-known lawyer, who'd later be appointed a federal judge, appears at your 341 meeting to ask two questions:

Lawyer: Mrs. Smith, where is your husband?

Mrs. Smith: In the country of Belize.

Lawyer: Can you tell me what he did with my client's $5,000,000?

Mrs. Smith: I don't know. Maybe you'll have to go to Belize and ask him.[8]

A third situation usually involves an angry ex-spouse or ex-business partner. In one case, an ex-wife came to the 341

---

[7] A purchase money security interest is typically an agreement to finance the purchase of an appliance or other good on a credit plan with the understanding that if you don't pay, the merchant will take back the item(s) in question. In the age of Amazon.com, this is a less common form of security interest. There are still local retailers who do this, however, and it comes up from time to time in the bankruptcy context.

[8] Although the names have been changed to protect the identities of the parties, this exchange actually happened at a meeting of creditors. My client had done nothing wrong—her ex-husband was the alleged crook.

meeting to reveal to the bankruptcy trustee the existence of assets that her husband had undervalued or had failed to disclose in his bankruptcy petition. In another example, two people entered into a partnership to run a nightclub. One partner took a lot of money and wasted it, and then that partner filed for bankruptcy. The other partner came to the 341 meeting to ask some very pointed questions about what his partner had done with all the money and whether there might be any left.

Although the bankruptcy Judge isn't involved at this point, the 341 meeting is a significant step in the bankruptcy process. If you fail to attend the 341 meeting, your bankruptcy will most likely be dismissed. Note too that you'll need to bring identification to this meeting, such as a driver's license, state-issued ID car, US passport, or military ID card. You'll also need to provide evidence of your Social Security number, either from the card itself or from forms such as a W-2 or tax return.[9]

3.4. Will you need debtor education after filing for bankruptcy?

Remember that the Bankruptcy Reform and Consumer Protection Act of 2005 imposed a requirement for pre-bankruptcy credit counseling. If you didn't get that counseling beforehand, your bankruptcy petition will be dismissed. The Bankruptcy Reform and Consumer Protection Act also imposes a requirement that after filing bankruptcy—but be-

---

[9] If you have issues concerning your identification or proving your Social Security number, talk to your attorney about them.

fore the case is completed—the debtor is required to take a one-hour financial management or debtor education class.

The purpose of this requirement as conceived by Congress was to try to equip debtors with information and tools that could prevent repeat bankruptcy filings. This requirement isn't much of a speedbump but does is increase the cost of bankruptcy. This course can cost as little as $10.00 or as much as $50.00 (depending on the provider), and couples can usually take it together for one fee. Like the credit counseling certificate, this course can also be completed online or over the phone. The financial management certificate you receive from the course is important because without it, your bankruptcy case will be closed without any discharge—and remember that the whole point of filing bankruptcy is to obtain a discharge. My advice is to take the course immediately after filing.

3.5. What is an adversary proceeding or bankruptcy lawsuit?

An adversary proceeding is a lawsuit in the bankruptcy court that deals with issues strictly related to bankruptcy law. I once had a client with a gambling problem. Gambling debts are dischargeable in bankruptcy, but what I didn't know was that a week before filing for bankruptcy, my client had gone down to our local Indian casino and taken a $5000 cash advance on his Discover Card. When using this example with clients, I tell them that this man had then "made some investments" and "had been unlucky in his investment strategy." These salient facts apparently escaped his attention.

When we filed his case a week later, he listed the debt but failed to mention to me how the debt had been incurred.

While the case was proceeding, I received a summons and complaint to deny the client's discharge as to the debt on the Discover Card. Why? The answer is that under the law, cash advances exceeding $750 taken within 70 days prior to filing for bankruptcy are deemed to be a nondischargeable debt.[10] In this instance, my client had to pay that money back, and we resolved the case by having him reaffirm the debt to Discover Card (remember that a reaffirmation agreement is a contract between the debtor and the creditor saying that both parties agree that the loan remains in effect and that the debtor will continue to make payments after bankruptcy.

Don't let this panic you. Creditors rarely if ever invoke this procedure (an adversary lawsuit). When they do, it's usually because the debtor has done something that violates bankruptcy law (as with the gambler above) or when a debtor's conduct is so dishonest that the creditor files suit to prevent that debtor from receiving a discharge at all. Remember—bankruptcy is a process for honest debtors. Those debtors who engage in fraud, theft, perjury, and intentional concealment of assets are the only ones at risk here—not you.

There are also situations when you as a debtor may file an adversary lawsuit against an abusive creditor: For example, when a creditor has willfully violated the automatic stay in bankruptcy (the automatic stay prevents creditors from attempting to collect debts from you as soon as you file for

---

[10] See 11 U.S.C. **Error! Main Document Only.**§ 523(a)(2)(c).

bankruptcy). This may be an action that you bring to prevent them from doing such a thing in the future and to seek damages for their unlawful conduct. Hence, adversary proceedings (bankruptcy lawsuits) aren't just for creditors—debtors can bring them too in order to protect themselves.

3.6. What is a means test?

Another aspect of the Bankruptcy Reform and Consumer Protection act of 2005 was the implementation of the means test. This is an analysis of gross income. If your gross income is over a certain amount, then you're not permitted to file for bankruptcy under Chapter 7. How do you pass the means test? We look at your last six months of income proceeding the month you're filing and determine your eligibility to file. While I can give you some rough numbers, there are a few variables that go into determining what your gross income is. For example, you can deduct certain expenses from your gross income, and the number of your dependents will also affect whether you're eligible to file for Chapter 7.

The US Justice Department has looked at every statistical census area in the United States and determined the cost of living in those areas. That impacts the means test and is thus part of the way eligibility for bankruptcy is determined. For example:

(See Median Income Table on the following page)

State of Washington, Benton County

Household Size	Median Annual Income	Median Monthly Income
1 Earner	$62,054	$5,171
2 People	$73,447	$6,121
3 People	$84,823	$7,069
4 People	$100,282	$8,357
5 People	$108,682	$9,057
6 People	$117,082	$9,757
7 People	$125,482	$10,457
8 People	$133,882	$11,157

U.S. Department of Justice Income Table 11/01/2017

If your calculated "median income" is close to or over the amount on the table, that doesn't automatically make you ineligible for Chapter 7 in and of itself. There are several other factors that affect your gross income. First, if you made most of your money in the first half of the year (more than six months ago—remember your median income is not based on what you made last year; it's based on what you made in the last six months). Second, some of your income may come from government sources, i.e., VA disability or Social Security. That income isn't included in your "median income" for purposes of means testing. If you have a family of four and the gross income of your household is under $100,000.00 per year, you can probably qualify to file for bankruptcy under Chapter 7.

3.7. Do you qualify to file for bankruptcy?

Congratulations, you've passed the means test, but the question remains: "Can I file for bankruptcy"? Are you a railroad, insurance company, or a bank? If not, then you can file for bankruptcy under Chapter 7 and Chapter 13. Do you have a mortgage in excess of $1.2 million? Well, you're not going to be eligible to file Chapter 13, but Chapter 7 is available. Do you have unsecured debts of more than $400,000.00? Again, you're not eligible for Chapter 13, but Chapter 7 is available.[11]

In fact, if you have that much debt, then it's probable that you're a physician, dentist, real estate developer, contractor, financial planner, business executive, entertainer, professional athlete, or other high-earning individual. Such people often don't qualify for Chapter 13 but may file for personal Chapter 11 bankruptcy. Normally, Chapter 11 is designed for large business organizations, but it can also be used by individuals, especially if they have a lot of debt and a lot of assets. Chapter 11 is the reorganization of last resort. Though complicated and expensive, Chapter 11 might be the right solution for a high-earning individual. Examples of people who've filed for Chapter 11 bankruptcy are the rapper 50 Cent, actor Burt Reynolds, interviewer Larry King, and boxer Mike Tyson.

There are other ways you might be ineligible for Chapter 7 too. Have you filed for bankruptcy before? Well, you can file bankruptcy as many times as you want, but there are

---

[11] As of April 1, 2016, if your secured debts are more than $1,184,200 or your unsecured debts are more than $394,725, then you're not eligible to file Chapter 13.

time limits between filings. if you've successfully completed a Chapter 7 case, you must wait eight years to file another Chapter 7 case and four years to file a Chapter 13 case. If you've successfully completed a Chapter 13 case, you'll need to wait two years to file another Chapter 13 case and four years to file a Chapter 7 case.[12]

3.8. What is the sequence of events in a bankruptcy case?

Pre-bankruptcy credit counseling (the 1st course);

Filing the bankruptcy petition and Chapter 13 plan;

Attendance at the 341 meeting (meeting of creditors);

Completion of the debtor education course (the 2nd course);

Bankruptcy Court hearing to confirm the proposed Chapter 13 plan of repayment;

Entry of an order confirming the Chapter 13 plan;

The debtor makes payments for 36 to 60 months per the plan;

After all the payments have been made, the court issues an order of discharge.

---

[12] If your prior bankruptcy case was dismissed by the court, and the dismissal was due to your failure to follow a court order, you may not be eligible to refile for six months from the date of that prior dismissal. Finally, you need to make sure that you're filing your bankruptcy in the correct place. This is called venue. To be eligible to file bankruptcy where you live, you need to have lived in that jurisdiction for at least six months (180 days).

4. What You Need to know about Bankruptcy Discharge and Why it's the Most Important Concept in this Book

If you're reading this book, it's highly probable that you're seeking a bankruptcy discharge, whether you know it or not. What you're trying to achieve is a discharge of your debts.

4.1. What is a bankruptcy discharge, and why do I want one?

In most individual bankruptcy cases—Chapter 7 as well as Chapter 13—the bankruptcy discharge is a court order that comes after all the requirements of the case have been completed. What does the discharge order actually mean? To put it in the simplest terms possible, it means that you're legally excused from paying the debts you had at the time you filed your bankruptcy petition. The discharge doesn't mean that you never incurred those debts or that they've been wiped away. Discharge simply relieves you of the legal duty to repay to those debts. The reason people file for bankruptcy is to get a fresh start. The bankruptcy discharge is that fresh start, and obtaining that discharge is the whole point of the bankruptcy process.

4.2. What is a "SUPER DISCHARGE"?

Bankruptcy Code section 11 USC § 523 defines debts that don't get discharged in bankruptcy. The obvious categories of non-dischargeable debts are certain taxes, debts incurred by fraud (i.e., you lied or misrepresented your financial condition to get a loan), child support and alimony, student loans (but see the section on student loans), willful and malicious injury to another person or property, criminal fines and restitution, and debts arising from drunk drivers who caused death or injury. This isn't a complete list—altogether, there are 19 categories of non-dischargeable debts. In Chapter 13, only eight of those categories apply, which means that the Chapter 13 discharge is broader than the discharge in Chapter 7. That's why the Chapter 13 discharge is sometimes called a "super discharge."

One example of debts that can't be discharged in Chapter 7 but that can be in Chapter 13 are some fines and penalties owed to governments. Note that criminal fines aren't discharged by any bankruptcy proceeding, but there are many government penalties that aren't criminal in nature, such as civil infractions (e.g., speeding, no proof of insurance, equipment violations, littering, and other non-criminal traffic violations). Those governmental penalties can be discharged under Chapter 13 (but not under Chapter 7).

This discussion isn't relevant unless I can demonstrate how ordinary people can benefit from Chapter 13's broader discharge. By way of example, I've had clients over the years who were not good drivers in their youth. In fact, they'd found themselves thousands of dollars in debt for criminal fines and civil infractions. Their driving privileges were suspended for non-payment of fines. In this instance, filing for Chapter 13 bankruptcy allows immediate reinstatement of the driver's license, reorganization of the criminal fines, and a discharge of all the civil infractions after completing the Chapter 13 repayment plan.

Other debts that can be eliminated by the "super discharge": Debts you incur to pay nondischargeable tax obligations (example: paying tax liabilities with a credit card) aren't dischargeable in Chapter 7 but are dischargeable in Chapter 13. Debts owed to a spouse, former spouse, or child through a divorce decree, or other related case (other than child support and alimony) are also dischargeable in Chapter 13 but not in Chapter 7. Other kinds of debts are also included in the "super discharge," but these are the ones most relevant to the average consumer debtor.

5. What You Need to Know about Liquidation and Reorganization and How Bankruptcy Works

5.1. What is the difference between liquidation and reorganization or "what is the difference between Chapter 7 and Chapter 13"? What is the difference between an asset and non-asset in bankruptcy cases or "please tell me what happens to my donut shop if I file for bankruptcy"?

There are only two types of bankruptcies that are common for most individual debtors—Chapter 7 and Chapter 13. The other chapters deal with different kinds of debtors: Chapter 9 is for governments (e.g., the City of Detroit), Chapter 11 for business entities (as noted above, this is usually for corporations such as United Airlines but sometimes high-earning individuals too), Chapter 12 for family farmers and commercial fishermen, and Chapter 15 for foreign entities.

For purposes of the people that I'm likely to represent, there are two concepts of bankruptcy that you should understand. The first is liquidation, and the second is reorganization.

5.2. Liquidation

Chapter 7 is sometimes referred to as a liquidation, whereas Chapters 11, 12, and 13 are reorganizations. Liquidation is a concept that involves selling assets and taking the proceeds of the sale to pay down debts. To demonstrate how liquidation works, let's assume that you're going to file for

Chapter 7 bankruptcy. When you file, everything you own ceases to belong to you and becomes the property of the bankruptcy estate. I like to think of the bankruptcy estate as a giant bowl into which you put everything you own. You may recall the man who owned a donut shop. I'd like you to have the donut shop in mind as I discuss the giant bowl (the bankruptcy estate) and your stuff (your property inside the bowl). Using your imagination and looking inside the bowl, what do you see? Your house, car, living room furniture, washer and dryer, stamp collection, closet full of clothes, retirement accounts, and of course that donut shop.

Although it's possible that some of the items in the bowl could be sold off to pay your creditors, it's likely that you'll be able to keep some or even all of them. As a debtor, you get something from the Bankruptcy Code called exemptions. The exact amount of those exemptions varies from state to state. In Washington, the exemptions can either be the ones found in 11 USC § 522 (the Federal Exemptions) or the ones in the Revised Code of Washington (State Exemptions). In Washington, you can choose either the federal exemptions or the state exemptions. Depending on your circumstances, one or the other set of exemptions may benefit you more.

What the exemptions allow you to do is to reach into the bowl (the bankruptcy estate) and start removing things to keep for yourself. Take your house, for example. What the bankruptcy court is concerned about is how much your house will sell for. If you have a mortgage and owe more money on your house than it's worth, then you don't need to exempt it. If you owe less than the total value of the house, you exempt your equity. For example, if the house is worth

$200,000 and your loan is $175,000, then you have $25,000 of equity to exempt, that is, to remove from the big bowl we call the bankruptcy estate.

By skillfully using your exemptions, you can keep your home, car, clothing, retirement accounts, stamp collection, furniture and appliances, etc. Again, you see why it's very important to hire a lawyer who's experienced in bankruptcy and understands these exemptions. One key reason not to represent yourself in a bankruptcy proceeding is that you want to be absolutely sure that you properly exempt your property. The law regarding exemptions is complex. Your attorney's job is to make sure that these exemptions are properly applied so as to avoid having your things sold off to repay creditors. A good bankruptcy lawyer will help you remove your stuff from the bowl (the bankruptcy estate) so that nothing you own gets sold off. However, if you happen to have a spare donut shop or an airplane or an oil well or a paid-for beach house, those items are likely to be sold off, no matter how skilled your attorney may be, due to the limits on exemptions.

5.3. Reorganization

The other concept in bankruptcy is reorganization. Instead of taking property out of the bowl and selling it, reorganization involves putting money or property into the bowl yourself for the bankruptcy trustee to distribute to creditors. In Chapter 13, you're proposing a plan of repayment over a 36- to 60-month timeframe. Imagine if you proposed to pay $25,000.00 into your Chapter 13 case, you would pay

$416.66 a month for 60 months (5 years). The Chapter 13 plan represents what you put into the bowl and will involve paying part or all of the amount you owe to creditors. After successfully completing the repayment plan, the court discharges any remaining amounts of the debts you owe.

This raises the question: Why would you do that (i.e., make payments for 3 to 5 years)? Well, there are some good reasons why. They include saving your home from foreclosure, getting your driver's license back, saving property from sale in a Chapter 7 bankruptcy, and discharging debts that can't be discharged in Chapter 7.

6. What You Need Know about Documents to Prepare Your Bankruptcy

I provide my clients a questionnaire and list of documents that will assist me in preparing the bankruptcy petition. Below is a list of items that I'll need in order to begin the process.

6.1. Do I need to provide a copy of my paystubs?

Yes, I need your pay stubs (also known as pay advices) going back at least six months. The reason for this is that the bankruptcy court looks at your income for the previous six months to determine what your annual income would be. If your gross income was $30,000.00 from July 1 to December 31, then on January 1st your annual income would be $60,000.00 for bankruptcy purposes. Previously, I discussed means testing. According to the U.S. Department of Justice's Income Table (see Chapter 3), an individual can earn up to $62,054.00 before exceeding the median income. Generally speaking, if your income is over the median for Chapter 7, you must file Chapter 13 instead.

Using the hypothetical income in the previous paragraph ($30,000.00 from July 1 to December 31), let's assume that you got a bonus of $20,000 in December. That would make your annual income $100,000 for bankruptcy purposes, even though you actually made only $80,000.00 for the whole year. In this hypothetical example, that would make you ineligible to file for Chapter 7 bankruptcy because your projected income based on the previous six months is more than $62,054.00

Using a different hypothetical example, assume that in the previous year you made $80,000.00, but instead of receiving your $20,000 bonus in December you received it in May. Your annual income for bankruptcy purposes would still be $60,000.00, even though you actually made $80,000.00. If you're asking why, it's again because income is only calculated looking back over the prior six months. This is why I always review my client's paystubs for that period, and how I determine if and when my clients will be eligible to file for Chapter 7 bankruptcy.

6.2. Do I need to provide my tax returns?

Yes, I require two years of tax returns. This is firstly because the bankruptcy trustee will want this information. Secondly, I use your returns to answer questions four and five on the statement of financial affairs (this is the list of questions following the schedules in the bankruptcy petition). These questions deal with income for the current year and the prior two years. The tax return is almost always the best way to determine gross income.

6.3. What if I don't have my tax returns?

There are three reasons why you may not have your tax returns. The first is that you've lost them. We can fix that by contacting the IRS and getting a tax transcript. That can take a couple of weeks because you may have to make a request to the IRS either online or by mail. The second reason you may not have tax returns is because your income is so low that you didn't have a reason to file one. In this case, we may provide a sworn statement explaining your situation to the court. The third reason you may not have tax returns is because you just haven't filed them. That situation is more problematic. It won't stop you from filing for bankruptcy, but it may prevent you from completing the case. The bankruptcy court will not confirm a Chapter 13 case unless all the pre-petition returns have been filed.

If you haven't filed your taxes for several years, the IRS will sometimes do it for you and will assess a tax obligation to you (this is not usually a good thing). When the IRS has assessed taxes to you, we may be able to get a tax transcript that will serve as a return for that year even if you haven't filed. Believe it or not, it's in your interest to file the returns even if you haven't done so for several years. Some of my clients have actually gotten tax refunds in this way or at least have had their tax debt reduced simply by filing those tax returns.

6.4. Why do you need my bank statements?

I'll ask you to provide your most recent bank statements. It's one way for me to determine or provide proof of your monthly income. It's also a way for me to spot unusual activity that could complicate your bankruptcy. I recently represented a client who qualified to file for bankruptcy. However, he had a purebred standard poodle that had just had puppies. He sold the puppies for a total of $7,000.00 but didn't tell me about it. His bank statements revealed this activity, and, ultimately, he had to wait to file for bankruptcy until he'd spent the money. Had we filed for bankruptcy immediately, the $7,000.00 could easily have been regarded as an asset that wasn't exempt and would've been demanded by the trustee and used to pay the man's debts. By waiting to file, my client was able to afford substantial dental work instead of losing that money to his creditors.

6.5. Will the bankruptcy trustee ask to see my bank statements?

The bankruptcy trustee will always require you to provide your bank statements. The trustee wants to review your bank records to make sure that the information in them is consistent with your bankruptcy petition. You'll need to include the statement that covers the date of your filing: For example, you file your case on May 31, but your bank statement runs from April 27 to May 28. You'd need to provide the statement from May 29 to June 29. It's important to remember that after the case is filed, you'll also need to provide the next month's bank statement as well.

6.6. What else will my attorney need in order to prepare my bankruptcy case?

Other than the paystubs, tax returns, and bank statements, there aren't usually any other documents I require before filing your bankruptcy case. Will I eventually need a list of your debts? Yes. More importantly, I'll need a good address for the creditors on that list. If you're self-employed, I might need your profit and loss statement or a list of business expenses. If we're having difficulty determining your personal expenses, then your utility bills and other monthly statements will help. I may need a copy of your lease agreement if you're renting an apartment or leasing a car. I'll need a copy of your property tax statement—first, to determine if you have a tax liability and, second, to determine the assessed value of the property, especially if the property is in another state and I can't get information about it online. If you've been divorced or have had a child support established, I may need a copy of any court orders (i.e., for divorce or establishing the child support). I'll certainly want to look at your divorce decree if it orders you to pay certain debts. Finally, if you have a child support obligation, I'll need the name and address of the person who receives child support. That person is legally entitled to notice of your bankruptcy case.

7. What You Need to Know about Chapter 13

From a bankruptcy lawyer's perspective, Chapter 13 is very similar to Chapter 7, with the exception that you have to prepare a Chapter 13 plan of repayment, and you then make payments to the Chapter 13 trustee for anywhere from 36 to 60 months. Most people would choose to file for Chapter 7 over Chapter 13. After all, it's a choice between having debts discharged in 90 to 120 days or being in bankruptcy for 3 to 5 years and continuing to make payments to creditors. Logic dictates that the less time spent in bankruptcy the better. Hence, Chapter 7 is usually preferable. Nevertheless, Chapter 13 might be for you. Here are ten common reasons people file for Chapter 13:

1. You're ineligible to file Chapter 7 because you make too much money.

2. You're ineligible to file Chapter 7 because you filed Chapter 7 less than eight years ago.

3. You're behind on your mortgage and you need to reorganize your finances to permit you to keep your home.

4. You need to invoke the automatic stay to get your automobile back from the repo man or to stop a home foreclosure, a garnishment, or even a lawsuit.

5. You want to keep an item of property that would otherwise have to be sold if you filed Chapter 7.

6. Your driver's license is at stake, and you need to reorganize and set up a payment plan in order to keep your license or get it back after it's been suspended.

7. You want to cramdown a loan. This means that you have a loan that has collateral, such as a car loan. Say you owe a lot more money on your car than it's worth. Chapter 13 will allow you to adjust the loan and only pay back the amount of the value of the collateral (i.e., the car is the collateral in this case)—that is a cramdown.

8. You need to repay certain debts and prevent creditors from going after an ex-spouse or other co-debtor. Chapter 13 has a unique feature called the co-debtor stay, which means that if you and your ex-spouse have a loan obligation together, your bankruptcy will protect that person even if he or she hasn't filed for bankruptcy.

9. You own a small business, and you want to continue operating that business while you're going through bankruptcy.

10. You need a broader discharge than you'd otherwise get in a Chapter 7 case.

7.1. What is a Chapter 13 plan?

A Chapter 13 plan is a document that sets out the terms of your reorganization. Some Chapter 13 plans are simple: a very basic statement of terms, e.g., how much money will be paid for how long and to whom. In this type of case, the court issues a detailed order outlining the rights, obligations, and terms to the creditors. Where I practice in the Eastern District of Washington, we have a district-specific plan. This plan is very detailed and outlines the terms, rights, duties, and obligations of the parties in interest (e.g., the debtors, creditors, trustee, etc.). Because this plan is so detailed, the court order approving it is a simple, one-sentence order: "The plan filed on [date] is confirmed."

7.2. What is a Chapter 13 confirmation hearing?

A proposed Chapter 13 plan must be approved by the bankruptcy judge before it can be "confirmed." If a plan is confirmed, then the confirmation is binding on all parties. That can be of tremendous benefit to the debtor, especially if the rights of creditors are significantly modified. For example, I was permitted to sue a bank holding a second mortgage for one of my clients. In that case, more money was owed on the first mortgage than the property was worth. In such circumstances, the law allows a debtor to sue a creditor to make a second mortgage an unsecured debt. After I sued the bank and got a judgment making the second mortgage an unsecured debt, the confirmed plan made that outcome binding. This meant that my client didn't have to pay the second mortgage at all when he completed his bankruptcy.

As you can imagine, interested parties (e.g., the debtor, the creditors, the bankruptcy trustee, etc.) may not approve of the plan and may have objections to its confirmation, especially when they might stand to lose a significant sum of money. In one case, I filed a lawsuit to make a second mortgage unsecured. The creditor objected to confirmation. Because the house in that case was actually worth more than we realized, the plan wasn't confirmed.

The most common objections to plans are usually made by the Chapter 13 trustee, whose job it is to collect and distribute the funds per the terms of the plan. Most of the trustee's objections pertain to the plan's legality and feasibility. Other objections are made by creditors who either have an interest in property or who object to the plan because it may discriminate against them. Finally, secured creditors (i.e., creditors who have an interest in collateral) have a right to be paid. They may be objecting because they want to get property back (e.g., a house or a car), or they want the court to protect their interests in property by requesting an order authorizing payment or requiring payment.

Before a plan can be confirmed, these disputes must be resolved. When the objection can't be resolved by agreement, the bankruptcy judge is the only person who can settle the disputes and confirm the plan.

7.3. What are some reasons why I wouldn't be able to file Chapter 13?

There are three reasons why you might be unable to file for Chapter 13 bankruptcy: 1) You have too much debt; 2) You received a discharge (via bankruptcy) within 4 years of filing; or 3) Your plan is not proposed in good faith.

Chapter 13 is for individuals, and there are limits to the amount of debt you can have. Remember, secured debts are debts that have collateral attached to them (e.g., mortgages and car loans). Debts that don't have collateral (e.g., credit cards, student loans, collection accounts, medical bills, etc.) are unsecured debts. If you have over $394,725.00 in unsecured debt (as of 2018), you cannot file Chapter 13. If you have $1,184,200.00 in secured debt (as of 2018), you can't file for Chapter 13 either. This means that you'll be required to file Chapter 7, or—if you absolutely must reorganize— Chapter 11 bankruptcy. In over 25 years of bankruptcy practice, I've only had one client who exceeded the debt limit in Chapter 13.

The second reason you might be ineligible is that you received a discharge recently. This does not prevent you from filing, but it does mean that you won't receive a discharge. If you filed for Chapter 7 and obtained a discharge already, you can still file a Chapter 13 reorganization. Why would you decide to do that if you can't get a discharge in Chapter 13? For example, you may have already gotten a discharge in Chapter 7, but you're now behind on your mortgage or another secured debt. You can still use Chapter 13 to stop a foreclosure and propose terms of repayment—thus saving your house, for example.

The third reason you might not be able to file for Chapter 13 is that your plan isn't one that's proposed in good faith or one that is imposed for an improper purpose. Bankruptcy is a process for honest debtors—not for those people who are attempting to hide assets or use the bankruptcy process to perpetrate a fraud (i.e., a debt incurred based on mis-representations of facts to a creditor). Such dishonesty isn't going to be permitted in Chapter 13, provided a creditor can demonstrate a lack of good faith.

8. What You Need to Know about Keeping Your Possessions

When I meet with prospective clients, the most common questions I hear are "Can I keep my car?" and "Can I keep my house?" As I said before, the answer to those questions is usually yes. However, just because you're filing for bankruptcy and you're going to get a discharge of your debts, that doesn't mean you're going to stop paying your mortgage or car payments—unless you don't want to keep the house or the car. Sometimes, we want debts to survive discharge because we want to keep the property/collateral that attaches to those debts. That is accomplished by use of a reaffirmation agreement (remember, a reaffirmation agreement is in essence an agreement in which you and a creditor agree that bankruptcy didn't occur between you).

8.1. Review—what is the bankruptcy estate?

You may remember that when you file for bankruptcy, everything that you own ceases to belong to you and becomes the property of the "bankruptcy estate." That includes every item of property you own, including copyrights, patents, intellectual property, stocks, bonds, bank accounts, tax refunds, business interests, etc. The bankruptcy estate is essentially an imaginary giant bowl where these things go until they are liquated (i.e., sold) to fund the bankruptcy or are exempted from sale in the bankruptcy petition (meaning that they're yours to keep).

8.2. Review—what is an exemption?

Exemptions are essential to the bankruptcy debtor. The exemptions determine which property you keep and which property is sold off. In Chapter 13, the exemptions are part of the process of determining how much you'll have to pay into your Chapter 13 plan. Again, if you think of the bankruptcy estate as a giant bowl, the exemptions are the way to remove your property from the bowl to keep.

8.3. Can I keep my car?

Yes, you usually can—but should you? Among the most common debts I see in bankruptcy are auto loans. In fact, some of the most important financial decisions people make are the purchase and financing of an automobile. Here are three common mistakes—but certainly not the only ones—that people make regarding cars and car loans:

> 1. You co-signed a car for a relative. That relative failed to pay, and now you're either paying for the car yourself or you're being sued for the repossession arrearage (remember Uncle Bob).[13]

> 2. You're a young, single person and have just gotten your first job. You went to a car dealership and

---

[13] A repossession arrearage is the remaining balance on an auto loan after the car has been repossessed and sold at auction. It's often the case that clients owe a repossession arrearage.

bought a brand-new Camaro, Mustang, or other highly-desirable vehicle. I once had a man come to see me who'd recently borrowed $70,000.00 to buy his "dream truck." It'd turned into a nightmare because it saddled him with a $1,200.00 monthly payment. Not only did he buy more vehicle than he could really afford, that vehicle depreciated (i.e., lost value) from the moment he drove it off the lot. [14]

3. You bought a used car from a dealer, and you financed the purchase either through the dealer or a bank. The car broke down soon after you brought it home. Since you bought the car "as is," there's no warranty. Now you find out the car needs a new engine, which is going to cost significantly more than the car is worth. You take the car back to the dealer and throw down the keys. You're then surprised when you get sued for the balance of the loan.

In bankruptcy, you can keep your car because you can usually exempt the equity. Often, cars have no value in bankruptcy because the debtor isn't the owner in a legal sense: While the registered owner is the debtor, the legal owner is the bank—and that's what counts. Only when a car is owned outright is there a risk that it'll have to be sold to pay creditors. The maximum amount of equity that an individual could theoretically exempt in a car (us-

---

[14] The rate of depreciation varies depending on the year, make, and model of the car. The first year always sees the greatest depreciation of the car's market value, with most cars losing about 20 percent or more of their original value. The loss continues year after year, with cars shedding about 60 percent of their original purchase price within the first five years of ownership.

ing the federal exemptions[15]) is $3,770.00 + $1,250.00 + $11,850.00 = $16,870.00. If you're filing as a married couple, that amount can go up to around $32,000.00, but that would also assume you don't own a home, and, all for practical purposes, you didn't have any property interests other than your car.

By the way, even if you own a car outright, it can often be exempted because the value isn't the price for which you'd buy it but rather the amount for which you could sell it to a dealer. We are looking largely at trade-in values not retail values. For example, I own a four-wheel drive 1992 Dodge pickup in good condition. If I saw this vehicle on a used car lot, I might expect to pay $2,500.00 for it. However, a dealer might only be willing to offer me $1,000.00. Thus, the value of the vehicle is $1,000.00, not $2,500.00 for your purposes here.

Another issue with cars and bankruptcy exemptions is when there are two or more vehicles. It's not difficult to exempt more than two vehicles when those vehicles have depreciated to a point where they have little value. However, if the cars are newer, in good condition, and have no loans against them, exempting more than two vehicles can become problematic.

Yet another problem is presented by collector vehicles. Only occasionally do clients have a classic car, perhaps one they restored or one they inherited. These types of vehicles can be worth a lot money and have the poten-

---

[15] See 11 U.S.C. § 522.

tial to be sold in the bankruptcy if they can't be exempted. Chapter 13 might offer a way for you to keep such a vehicle for yourself.

8.4. Can I keep my house?

Yes, usually you can keep your home thanks to what is known as a homestead exemption. In Florida and Texas, there are unlimited homestead exemptions. You could have a $10,000.000.00 house, then file for Chapter 7 bankruptcy and still keep that house. Most states aren't so generous but still do allow you to choose between using the state exemption and the federal exemption. Washington is such a state.[16] The federal exemptions are: $23,675.00 for an individual and $47,350.00 for married couples (note that this is double the exemption allowed an individual). The Washington State homestead exemption is $125,000.00. You might have a house that is worth $250,000.00, but if you owe $200,000.00 on it, you can exempt all that equity in Chapter 7 using the Washington State homestead exemption.

8.5. Reaffirming Debts

What does it mean to reaffirm a debt, and what does it have to do with keeping your things? As a reminder, a reaffirmation agreement is a contract between you and a credi-

---

[16] Other states, such as Tennessee, don't permit this choice. If you file in the Volunteer State, you must use that state's homestead exemption, which is among the least generous in the country: You can only exempt up to $5,000 of equity in your home (increasing to $7,500 for joint owners and $25,000 if you have at least one minor child).

tor. This is usually a secured creditor (but can also be an unsecured creditor). In effect, you say, "Mr. Banker, let's pretend that I didn't file for bankruptcy, and we'll sign a contract stating that neither your rights as to my loan or my rights and duties as to the loan change. Let's just keep everything the way it was before I filed my case."

The bankruptcy discharge excuses you from paying debts you had prior to filing the case. If you don't have a reaffirmation agreement, then you have no obligation to pay that debt. When this involves a car, reaffirmation is important because if you have a secured debt on a car, and you don't reaffirm it, the creditor doesn't have an obligation to allow you to keep the car. Creditors can, and sometimes do, repossess cars in these circumstances. In fact, they may even refuse your payments to them if the debt is not reaffirmed.

Houses are another matter. The foreclosure process is different from the mere repossession of a vehicle. Even if you have no obligation to make payments on a home, you'll want to continue to make those payments to keep that home. Otherwise, the bank will eventually start the process of foreclosure. The bank retains its interest in the property, and although you might not be obligated to pay the debt, the bank retains the right to take the property if it doesn't receive payments. If you haven't reaffirmed your home loan, the bank will still accept your payment, but (because you have no obligation to pay the bank) it won't report your payments for credit reporting purposes.

8.6. Assuming Leases

A lease contract for a vehicle or a lease on an apartment usually needs some acknowledgement in the bankruptcy court so that the contract or lease will continue. This is because the debtor has the right to walk away from the lease when you file for bankruptcy. While it may make financial sense to walk away from an auto lease, some clients opt to assume them instead. With home or apartment leases, an order assuming the lease protects the debtor from rent increases or termination of their lease (for the remainder of the term of the lease). Otherwise, that lease becomes a month-to-month tenancy, and the debtor is then vulnerable to rent increases and even termination of their tenancy.

8.7. What happens if I win the lottery or if my Aunt Millie leaves me a million dollars the day after I file for bankruptcy?

Some things you can't keep. The Bankruptcy Code has a six-month look-back. If you receive a big windfall (either money or property) with six months of filing for bankruptcy, it must go into the bankruptcy estate's big bowl for repaying creditors. Remember that if this happens, you need to be honest and report it. If you don't, there will be civil consequences in the bankruptcy court, and you may have criminal liability as well.

Books can and have been written solely on the topic of non-dischargeability. The purpose of this book is to answer basic bankruptcy questions and address the concerns of the average consumer debtor. This section aims to familiarize the reader with the concept of non-dischargeability and to discuss what is and isn't dischargeable in a general manner.

As previously stated, Bankruptcy Code section 11 USC § 523 defines debts that don't get discharged. Again, the obvious categories of non-dischargeable debts are certain taxes, along with debts incurred by fraud (i.e., you lied or misrepresented your financial condition to get a loan), child support and alimony, student loans (but see the section on student loans), willful and malicious injury to another person or property, criminal fines and restitution, and debts arising from drunk drivers who caused death or injury. Again, there are 19 categories of non-dischargeable debts that apply in Chapter 7 but only eight in Chapter 13 (hence the "super discharge").

9.1. What are the debts that you can usually discharge in bankruptcy?

Rather than focusing on what isn't dischargeable in bankruptcy, the question I get most frequently from prospective clients is, "Mr. McBurney, can I bankrupt X?" Sometimes people are concerned about collections, garnishments, lawsuits, and judgments. Since the Bankruptcy Reform Act of

2005, I've come across many prospective clients who are confused about what is and isn't dischargeable. The following can usually be discharged: doctor bills, hospital bills, business debts, auto loans, repossession arrearages, credit card bills, payday loans, bad checks (if not made with the intent to defraud), personal loans, debts to relatives, gambling debts, and much, much more. I've had clients who mistakenly believed that if a court issues a judgment against them, then that particular debt can't be discharged. Sometimes, clients have had collectors lie to them by saying they can't file for bankruptcy. The fact is that what can be discharged is very broad, and what is not dischargeable is limited to what is in the Bankruptcy Code (11 USC § 523).

9.2. What are the debts that you can sometimes discharge in bankruptcy?

We've previously discussed the "super discharge" available in Chapter 13. That is indeed a broader discharge than in Chapter 7. For example, debts stemming from injuries you caused to others might not be discharged in Chapter 7 but are discharged in Chapter 13. Debts to governmental units for fines and penalties are dischargeable in Chapter 13 but not Chapter 7. Contrary to what many people believe, overpayments from the government are one type of debt that can be discharged in both Chapter 7 and Chapter 13. If the government made a mistake and overpaid unemployment or labor and industry benefits, this is an actual pecuniary loss ("pecuniary" is the term used in the code and simply means having to do with money). it's a situation in which the government is not fining you but instead lost money by no fault of yours. That gets discharged in Chapter 7.

Many people have the misconception that when you owe money to the government, you can't discharge the debt. There are in fact many instances when you can. You can even discharge income taxes. This is because not all income taxes are non-dischargeable or entitled to priority (priority means that the taxes get paid before other debts as long as there is money in the bankruptcy estate). Usually, income taxes and other taxes entitled to priority aren't dischargeable. However, if a tax is not entitled to priority in the Bankruptcy Code (11 USC § 507), you may be able to discharge it.

There are several factors that go into determining the dischargeability of income taxes: 1) You must have filed a return; 2) The taxes must be over three years old; and 3) You must have filed that tax return at least nine months prior to filing for bankruptcy. That's another reason why you need to make sure to file your tax returns. If you don't, then your tax obligation is never dischargeable.

One thing to keep in mind is that the IRS only seeks to collect taxes for a ten-year period. If you still owe your 2007 taxes for some reason and it's now 2018, the IRS will have stopped collecting, unless your property is subject to a tax lien (in that case, collection can be extended either by the taxpayer or by operation of law). Please note, however, that the time for collection of back taxes is extended by filing for bankruptcy. This is due to the fact that filing for bankruptcy "tolls" the statute of limitations (meaning that it stops the collection clock) for the period of time that the taxpayer's bankruptcy case is active.

9.3 Can student loans ever be discharged?

Contrary to popular belief, student loans can indeed be discharged—however, it takes a lawsuit to do it. The debtor must demonstrate that if the student loan debt isn't discharged, it'd lead to an undue hardship on the debtor and the debtor's dependents. More specifically, here's what needs to be demonstrated at trial to discharge student loans: 1) The debtor can't maintain, based on current income and expenses, a "minimal" standard of living for the debtor and the debtor's dependents if forced to repay the student loans; 2) Additional circumstances exist indicating that this state of affairs is likely to persist for a significant portion of the student loan repayment period; and 3) The debtor has made good faith efforts to repay the loans. This is called the *Brunner* test[17] and is used in most U.S. Bankruptcy Courts to determine if a student loan can be discharged.

9.4. What kinds of debts can never be discharged?

In order for a debt not to be dischargeable, the court will have to make a determination as to dischargeablity in many instances. This is usually done in an adversary lawsuit brought by a creditor or other interested party. Some people do have debts that aren't dischargeable. For example, maybe

---

[17] *Brunner v. New York State Higher Educ. Servs. Corp.*, 831 F. 2d 395 (2d Cir. 1987).

you overstated your income on a loan application or there were questions about whether a debt was incurred by some other fraudulent means.

Even if there are real facts that could be brought to the attention of the bankruptcy court to prove non-dischargeablity, if no objection to the debt is brought by a creditor, it'll usually get discharged anyway. There are numerous kinds of debts that on their face aren't dischargeable (in Chapter 7, this includes fines and penalties to governmental units as well as Homeowner's Association Dues; in both Chapters 7 and 13, there are student loans). Furthermore, there are four categories of debts that are never discharged and usually don't require a lawsuit to establish that fact: 1) child support and alimony, 2) fines, penalties, and restitution you owe for breaking the criminal law, 3) taxes entitled to priority, and 4) debts arising out of someone's death or injury as a result of drunk driving.

9.5. What about debts that are suspending my driver's license?

Remember that traffic fines and penalties as well as other debts owed to governments (excluding taxes, criminal fines, and restitution) can be discharged in Chapter 13. Often, these debts cause suspension of a driver's license for non-payment. Also dischargeable in both Chapters 7 and 13 are debts incurred in auto accidents (not involving drunk driving). The most common scenario is when my prospective client's license is suspended due to criminal traffic fines, infractions, and Washington's financial responsibility law (that law suspends a license when a driver doesn't have insurance and hasn't satisfied damages caused by an accident). This debt can be discharged in Chapter 7, and a bankruptcy filing will be sufficient to get the Department of Licensing to reinstate the license.

Clients benefit from Chapter 13's broader discharge as to traffic and civil infractions. As we know, government penalties aren't always criminal in nature—there are also civil infractions: e.g., speeding, no proof of insurance, equipment violations, littering, and other non-criminal traffic violations. A Chapter 13 bankruptcy filing is what is needed to get the Department of Licensing to reinstate the license.

While criminal fines aren't dischargeable in any bankruptcy, a Chapter 13 plan can provide for repayment of those fines as part of the process of reorganizing the debtor's finances, and the criminal fines can be paid according to the plan. The bottom line is that bankruptcy permits the debtor to get his driver's license back, which is part of the process of getting a fresh start for the honest debtor.

9.6. How does bankruptcy deal with taxes, fines, fees, and overpayments from the government?

We've discussed these subjects previously. Suffice it to say that income taxes aren't dischargeable unless they're over three years old and a return has been filed at least nine months prior to filing for bankruptcy (even then there are exceptions to this rule, especially when the IRS assesses a tax liability to you before you've filed a late return, which means that the debt is not dischargeable in that case).

Fines and penalties that aren't criminal are dischargeable in Chapter 13. This applies to more than just traffic fines; other civil penalties are included too. Finally, overpayments by the government to you are discharged in both Chapter 7 and Chapter 13 as long as the debt is an actual pecuniary loss (again, meaning a loss having to do with money—but not a penalty or fine that had been imposed on you).

10. What You Need to Know about Representing Yourself

Some people choose to represent themselves in bankruptcy without an attorney. In fact, about 28 percent of filings are made by people going it alone. This kind of debtor is known as a "*pro se* debtor." It could be the case that the *pro se* debtor just doesn't have the money to hire a lawyer or has a very simple case and has spent time reading books, visiting law libraries, buying or downloading forms (and filling them out). The *pro se* debtor will need to prepare all the forms correctly, take those forms to the bankruptcy court and file them, attend the meeting of creditors, and represent himself or herself before the bankruptcy court.

It's not impossible to do all that, but it isn't advisable. My first bankruptcy case was back in 1992, when I was working for a lawyer in Seattle. In those days, we were just beginning to get computer software to make the process simpler. My employer was very old school (no computers). I was handed a thick stack of forms—remember the bankruptcy petition is a 50- to 70-page document (and that hasn't changed since the 1990s). Working a couple of hours per day at a typewriter, it took me a full two weeks to prepare a relatively simple bankruptcy petition. While computers do make this process easier today, there still remains the steep learning curve when preparing all the forms. If you're representing yourself, you'll face that steep learning curve, and you most likely won't have the benefit of a law degree.

10.1. Why is representing yourself in a bankruptcy case usually a bad idea?

Even if you have a simple case, bankruptcy can be an intimidating and time-consuming process. Remember that when hiring a lawyer for Chapter 7, you're paying primarily for his expertise in drafting the petition correctly and guiding you through the process. Going it alone means that you'll need to research the law, fill out all those forms accurately, and attend hearings. If you're not comfortable with any aspect of the bankruptcy process, you should consider hiring an attorney who'll prepare the forms, attend the hearings with you, and guide you through the process.

Also, when you represent yourself, you'll be held to the same standard as a lawyer. Chapter 13 bankruptcy has always been more complex than Chapter 7. While you might be able to represent yourself in a simple Chapter 7 case, a recent study in the US Bankruptcy Court for the Central District of California demonstrated that less than one percent of *pro se* debtors in Chapter 13 cases were able to get the court to confirm their bankruptcy plans. Even experienced lawyers may need to amend a Chapter 13 plan more than once to get it confirmed, and even after confirmation, the lawyer may have to amend the plan again to keep the case moving forward (e.g., to get the client a discharge). You might be able to change the spark plugs in your car and even repair the gaskets and seals, but unless you're a skilled mechanic, you shouldn't attempt to rebuild an automatic transmission on your own.

11. What You Need to Know about Alternatives to Bankruptcy

As I mentioned at the beginning of the book, bankruptcy is not always necessary and sometimes not even in your interest. There are alternatives to bankruptcy that you can and should consider, depending on your specific circumstances.

11.1. Why might someone choose to do nothing?

As previously stated, doing nothing is not usually the best option. However, there are debtors who are "judgment proof," meaning that there's no way for a creditor to collect from them. This is normally the case with people whose sole source of income is Social Security or disability benefits. These benefits are not generally subject to garnishment or wage assignment (child support may be the rare exception to that rule).

The other type of debtor who might consider doing nothing is someone who has debts but whose creditors have taken no action, that is, there are no lawsuits or other activities by creditors. As the old saying goes, "Let sleeping dogs lie." If you don't, then you just might get bitten.

If you aren't working and don't have any property, then bankruptcy may not be necessary. I've had clients who've come to me to file for bankruptcy and who then decided to wait after hearing my advice about their situation. Sometimes, I've met with clients and didn't see them again for a year before they finally decided to file their case. Your circumstances might dictate that you should file your case as soon as possible—but unless you're facing a lawsuit, foreclosure, or garnishment, you may not require a bankruptcy filing this very minute. Make sure you take time to consider your options. You shouldn't be pressured into filing for bankruptcy. Do it because it's the right decision for you.

11.2. How do state law statutes of limitations impact my decision to file for bankruptcy?

I discussed statutes of limitations earlier. I think it's important to touch on them again. For a prospective bankruptcy client's purposes, the statute of limitation is the period of time in which a creditor has to act before a debt becomes uncollectible. Statutes of limitations vary from state to state. Here are the most relevant ones for Washington State:[18]

1. <u>Two years</u> for libel, slander, assault, or false imprisonment. For example, say you were in a fight at a bar and you hit someone. That person had to go to the hospital and get stitches. This would be an assault.[19] The person who was assaulted would have two years from the date of the bar fight to sue you to collect his or her medical bills and other damages (such as pain and suffering). Note: These kinds of debts may be non-

---

[18] For statutes of limitations, see RCW § 4.16.100.

[19] Please note that the exact legal definitions of crimes such as assault vary from state to state.

dischargeable in Chapter 7 cases, per 11 USC § 523 (a)(6), if the action in question was willful and malicious.

2.   Three years for oral contracts and for waste or trespass on real property, and negligence. For example, you're hired to paint somebody's house. You agreed to a price, painted the house, but you didn't get paid. Because your agreement to paint the house wasn't in writing, your contract is only an oral contract. In this case, you have three years to take the owner of the house to small claims court (with a written contract, you'd have six years). If you're in a car accident and crashed into a fence, the owner of the fence has three years to sue you to collect the damages for negligence. Again, willful and malicious damages (e.g., trespass to real property) aren't dischargeable in Chapter 7 cases, per 11 USC § 523 (a)(6).

3.   Five years for actions to recover real property improperly sold by a guardian, personal representative of an estate, or an executor. For most people considering bankruptcy, it's unlikely that this situation would occur.

4.   Six years for actions on contracts that are in writing and accounts receivable. Contracts are generally self-explanatory (e.g., a purchase and sale agreement, a loan, a promissory note, an agreement to provide services in exchanges for money, etc.). Most people have a basic familiarity

with contracts, and so I won't go into detail about them here. However, an account receivable is something different and relevant enough to prospective bankruptcy filers that this limitation on action requires more explanation.

If you lived in a town with a general store and bought things from that store on an account, you might not have an actual written contract. Because it was an account that you paid fully or in part each month, it would be an account receivable. For most consumer debtors in the 21st century, the accounts receivable statute of limitations applies only to credit cards. Certainly, you may have contracted for that credit card years and years ago (e.g., American Express, John Doe member since 1992). Note that the balance on a credit card account is considered an account receivable. According to the law, the statute of limitations for credit card debt doesn't start when you signed the account agreement but when you last made a payment on the account. Assume that it's 2018, and you have an American express account on which you owe $10,000.00. You last made a payment on that account in 2013. Further, assume you were persuaded to make a payment on that account on December 31, 2017—just shy of the six-year anniversary of the last time you made a payment in 2013. Because credit card debts qualify as account receivables, the statute of limitation resets every time you make a payment. Therefore, making a payment in December of 2017 resets the statute of limitation just before the account would've become uncollectible.

5.   10 years for judgments. If you're successfully sued, the party who obtained a judgment against you has 10 years to collect the judgment. However, 90 days before that 10-year period is up, a motivated creditor can apply to the court to have the judgment extended for an additional 10 years.

If you have a significant debt that is close to the end of its statute of limitations, you may want to wait and see if someone actually sues you. Also, if someone has a judgment against you, you should check how long it has been since the court issued the judgment. If you're close to the end of the statute of limitation, it may make sense to wait it out and see if the debt becomes uncollectible. You may then be able to avoid bankruptcy.

11.3. What is a debt management plan?

A debt management plan is not a consolidation loan; in most senses, it's similar to Chapter 13 bankruptcy. In debt management scenarios, you enter into an agreement to repay your debts over a 3- to 5-year period. Such plans begin when you contact a debt management company. Usually, this company is a nonprofit organization that advertises itself as a debt relief organization. Before choosing a particular debt management program, a prospective debtor will want to research that company strenuously and look to see if there have been complaints about its performance. If you've found a good debt management company and you enter it's program, the company will contact all your creditors and attempt to negotiate reductions in interest rates, fees, and payments in exchange for partial or full repayment (depending on your circumstances). The debt management program will then package this for you and set up a single monthly payment that comes out of your checking account.

Debt management is very similar to Chapter 13 but without any of the advantages offered by Chapter 13. You won't be able to impose terms of repayment on your creditors. Nor are your creditors prevented from suing you if they change their minds. Furthermore, you don't get the benefit of the Chapter 13 super discharge.

Frankly, I'm skeptical of debt management programs because they're an inferior solution compared to bankruptcy. Yet, for the right individual, especially someone who wants to avoid bankruptcy or can't file for bankruptcy, debt management might be preferable to having to deal with your creditors individually.

11.4. How could negotiating with creditors be an alternative to bankruptcy?

In the right circumstances, negotiating with creditors is preferable to filing for bankruptcy. During the financial crisis following 2008, many people struggled due to unemployment and the crash in the housing market. I had a former college classmate contact me for help negotiating with creditors. I advised him that he could file for bankruptcy, but he felt very strongly about paying his debts. He had about $40,000 in credit card bills and only $25,000.00 in cash. I began the process of negotiating with his creditors. Some were willing to take less than the face value of what the man owed. In one case, a creditor agreed to settle a $10,000.00 debt for a mere $1,700.00. Another creditor was firmer and held out for 50 cents on the dollar. In the end, we settled all his accounts. We obtained all the settlements in writing. Each transaction was well documented, especially the ones that were settled for less than the full amount of the debt, which provided him with proof in case a creditor later tried to renege on a settlement.

While this debtor could've discharged all his debts in bankruptcy, he wanted to avoid it and pay what he could. I was glad I could help him. In the right set of circumstances, you may also want to negotiate with your creditors, especially when you have only a few debts, and you have money to work out a settlement for less than full value.

11.5. The "Dave Ramsey" approach—bankruptcy as a last resort?

You may be familiar with popular radio host Dave Ramsey. He wrote the book *The Total Money Makeover*, and through his company, he sponsors a program called Financial Peace University, which is held at churches and other locations around the country. Mr. Ramsey doesn't like bankruptcy. He had to file for bankruptcy himself many, many years ago, and it was a difficult, emotionally-painful experience for him. Owing to that experience, he strongly encourages people to develop a budget, live within their means, and avoid borrowing money. His approach to repaying debts is to list your debts from smallest to largest. Then, you should pay the smallest one first and work your way up to the largest, just as if you're eating elephant, one bite at a time. The benefit of this program is that people who can follow this approach develop the necessary financial discipline they need to be successful with money. Dave's advice is very sensible. If everyone followed that advice, I'd be out of a job.

When you go through the process of repaying your debt—when you develop the discipline to budget your money and control your spending—you can be financially successful in the future. While as a bankruptcy practitioner I can get you a fresh start, it's not necessarily the case that I'm doing you a favor. This is especially true if you don't learn to master the financial disciplines of budgeting, repaying your debts, and staying out of debt in the first place. Not learning these things means setting yourself up for failure. I've had clients who came to me to file for bankruptcy and then were right back in my office to file bankruptcy again eight years later (which is the minimum interval allowed with Chapter 7). Sometimes, the need to file for bankruptcy a second time is due to events beyond a person's control, such as unforeseen medical expenses and changes in personal circumstances. Just as often, however, the situation is due to poor financial habits and poor discipline. I'd gladly do a bankruptcy for you. I'd also gladly be of service to you in the future. However, I'd hope that if I do file your bankruptcy, you'll learn to avoid debt, follow a budget, keep track of your money, develop financial discipline, and become financially successful.

12. What You Need to Know to Decide if Bankruptcy is for You

Filing for bankruptcy is an individual decision. It may be the best decision you've ever made, or it may not be right for you. In the following paragraphs, I've posed questions you should ask yourself if you're considering bankruptcy.

12.1. Are you eligible to file for bankruptcy?

The first question I ask a prospective client is, "Have you ever filed for bankruptcy before?" If the answer is yes, then I calculate how long it's been since the prior case was filed or was discharged. If a prospective client filed a previous Chapter 7 case, I go out eight years from the date of the prior filing. If the prospective client is going to file a Chapter 13 case, I look back four years from when their last bankruptcy was discharged.

Another question is whether or not a prospective client has lived in the judicial district for at least six months. For example, if you lived in Idaho and moved to Washington just this month, and you asked me to file your bankruptcy, I'd have to refer you to an Idaho attorney. Why? Because where you file your case is based on where you've lived for the last six months (180 days).[20]

---

[20] Note that this 180-day residency requirement applies to individuals; venue and eligibility issues are different for corporations and other entities.

12.2. Do you think your financial situation is going to improve in the near future?

In this book, I've discussed alternatives to bankruptcy. It may very well be that your situation was caused by a temporary setback or one-time event. If you're going back to work, or your financial situation will improve in some other way, you may find yourself with increased cash flow. In that case, a certain amount of budgeting and discipline will allow you to recover your financial footing. Conversely, it may be the case that the debts incurred when you were in the middle of the financial storm are so large that paying them off would be impracticable. Sitting down with a good bankruptcy attorney will help you wade through these options and determine whether improved circumstances will allow you to avoid bankruptcy or whether filing for bankruptcy makes sense.

12.3. Are most of your debts unsecured and hence could possibly be discharged?

What kind of debts do you have? Recently, I met with prospective clients who thought they'd achieved the American dream. They had two kids, a house, two new cars, and a combined income of about $8,000.00 a month. Yet, they were always broke and didn't understand why. They wanted a fresh start via bankruptcy. Between them, they had $169,000.00 in student loans. They also owed $200,000.00 on a home mortgage, $50,000.00 in car loans, and $10,000.00 in credit card debt. Their total indebtedness was thus about $429,000.00. As their student loan obligations were coming due and could no longer be deferred, a significant portion of their monthly budget was taken up repaying those student loans. Because student loan debts aren't dischargeable except under certain circumstances, filing for bankruptcy would've been only of marginal benefit to them. This was especially the case because they were unwilling to return the cars to the bank or walk away from their home. Bankruptcy would've discharged only about $10,000.00 worth of credit card debt. These prospective clients left my office angry and unsatisfied because bankruptcy wouldn't help them hardly at all.

Bankruptcy does offer a fresh start for most people, but students need to be very cautious about going into debt for school. You might find yourself with a degree in history along with $100,000.00 of non-dischargeable student loans that prevent you from moving forward with your life—getting married, buying a home, and starting a family. Too much student loan debt creates *de facto* indentured servants. You might be able to get a degree, but unless you pay back your student loans, you become a slave to Uncle Sam.

12.4. Are you willing to accept bankruptcy's negative impacts?

You must understand that bankruptcy will remain on your credit report for ten years. Also, court records are public records. This can come back to bite you in unexpected ways. For example, if you're running for city council or another public office, your opponent might try using your bankruptcy filing against you even if it happened a long time ago. If your job is a position of trust (i.e., you work for a bank or other financial institution) and your bankruptcy case undermines that position of trust (especially if the bank or credit union you work for lost money because of your bankruptcy), you may find yourself out of work. If you're in the military or in a sensitive government position (i.e., you have a top-secret security clearance), a bankruptcy filing may affect your continued employment as well.

It should be no surprise that bankruptcy will negatively affect your credit score. It'll be more difficult—but not impossible—to get a mortgage or borrow money for other purposes. According to the Home Buying Institute, it can take one to four years after bankruptcy before a debtor can get approved for a mortgage loan. Federal Housing Authority (FHA) applicants must wait two years from the end of bankruptcy before they can apply for an FHA loan. Expect to pay higher interest rates for the credit you do get. As your credit score improves over time, you can get better interest rates, but you'll still be paying higher rates than non-bankruptcy filers.

After completing your bankruptcy case, you'll begin getting credit card offers immediately. Avoid these offers because they come with high annual fees and very high interest rates. Credit card companies aren't stupid—they know that even the riskiest of borrowers are worth taking a chance on because: 1) It's unlikely that you'll file for bankruptcy again for at least eight years; and 2) They can charge higher rates for interest and fees.

12.5. Do you have any other good options?

Can you work your way out of your debts, or do you really need a fresh start? From time to time, I meet new clients who have $5,000.00 to $10,000 in debt. I often advise these people that bankruptcy is not in their best interest. The exception is when there's no other way to break a catch-22 situation without filing for bankruptcy. For example, a client has lost his job because his driver's license is suspended, and having that license was required by his employer. The suspension was due to an uninsured auto accident. That auto accident left my client with a $9,000.00 debt. Under Washington State's Financial Responsibility Law, that debt must be paid before his license will be reinstated. This client's catch-22 situation works like this: 1) My client has a debt; 2) That debt suspends his driver's license; 3) He loses his job because he can't drive; 4) He needs to pay the debt to clear his license; 5) He needs a new job to pay the debt; 6) He can't get a new job because he needs his driver's license. We are now back to square one. If my client can't borrow the money to settle his debt, then it's the case that bankruptcy is his best option even though he owes less than $10,000.00.

12.6. Are you comfortable walking away from your financial obligations?

Bankruptcy does have a personal, emotional impact. For some, it's an admission of failure, for others there may be deeply-held convictions of a religious nature or of some other kind about paying one's debts. This is the case even though society is much more understanding about these things than in the past. While we've talked about the negative financial impacts of bankruptcy, there are personal and social impacts too. These arise more from how we see ourselves, rather than how others see us. You may or may not realize that newspapers publish the names of people who file for bankruptcy. Some clients want to know what they can do to avoid having their names published. One client of mine was so concerned about this that he waited to file his bankruptcy until he'd moved to another town so as to avoid having his name in the local paper.

However, most people will never know about your bankruptcy case, and most people won't care. I myself hardly read the local paper anymore and never page through the bankruptcy notices. Moreover, I've never looked down on someone else because he or she needed to file for bankruptcy. If you're an honest debtor who's caught in a financial storm, bankruptcy is what you need in order to get a fresh start. We have the bankruptcy system for a reason. We don't want people to be crushed by debt for life. This is why the U.S. Constitution allows it. There's no shame in using a system that lets people recover from financial disaster and begin anew. Accept things for what they are, reflect on how you can change your habits for the better, and develop the financial discipline you need for a debt-free future.

13. What You Need to Know about Collection Agencies and Credit Card Companies

The three most common debt problems I see are credit card debt, medical bills, and collections. Credit cards become a problem when your income doesn't allow you to pay more than the minimum monthly payments. Once you're delinquent on your credit cards, the credit card companies start calling you, sometimes daily, at home and even at work. After about four months without payment, these accounts may be turned over to a third-party collector. That collector will also call you, send you letters, as well as threaten to take you to court and garnish your wages/bank accounts.

Collection agencies will write, call, text, sue, and generally make themselves a nuisance. I often consult with people who're considering bankruptcy because they can't handle all the letters and phone calls. One reason for hiring a lawyer is to get the collectors to stop calling you. The Fair Debt Collection Practice Act (FDCPA) lays out the rights consumers have when dealing with third-party collections agencies. One very important right you have is this: When you're represented by an attorney, you can require that the collectors contact your lawyer instead of you. That stops the harassment.

13.1. Are collection agencies "lying liars who tell lies"?

In short—yes, they are. Everything that collectors do when speaking with you on the phone or contacting you by mail is designed to get you to make a payment. Dealing with collection agencies is frustrating and difficult, all the more so because you may not be in the best place emotionally during the financial storm. Here is a little hypothetical conversation:

Collector: This is Johnny Bosadova from the collection agency. This is an attempt to collect a debt. Anything you say during this conversation will be used for that purpose. You haven't made a payment on your bill, and now it's 90 days past due. What kind of loser are you that you don't pay your bills?

You: Hey, I lost my job, and I don't have any money. I just need a little slack until I can find some work.

Collector: Listen, dirt bag, you'd better pay this bill. We're authorized to garnish your bank account. If I don't receive a payment today, we'll remove the funds from your account tomorrow.

You: Hey, my rent money is all that's in my account right now....

Collector: You need to pay your debt—your rent isn't important. Your need to make payments on this debt, otherwise I'm escalating this to our collection action team....

While the foregoing is not an actual conversation, it's not untypical of the strategies employed by commercial collectors. They want you to get emotional and make a bad decision (e.g., pay them instead of paying your rent). While some collection agencies are professional, others do employ hardball tactics and do lie to consumers to get them to cough up the money they owe. Those lies include things like this:

You: I owe you $5000.00. If I pay you $500.00 will settle that settle the debt?

Collector: Sure, I can do that, I just need your bank account to take a payment over the phone.

Unless you got the debt settlement agreement in writing, the collector is just going to call you back next month to demand payment on the remaining balance of the debt. Furthermore, with your bank account information, the collector may try to garnish the account. A collector must get a court judgment to garnish wages or bank accounts. Collectors often lie about this by telling people that they're going to garnish wages or bank accounts when they haven't actually gone to court. Also, you may get sued, especially if the debt is for medical bills. Don't ignore your mail or ignore process servers. If you do, a judgment may be entered against you in favor of the collection agency because you didn't respond to the lawsuit (usually, you should respond). Always consult a lawyer when you're being sued. A judgment might be avoided simply by responding to the suit and working with your attorney.

13.2. Why trying to make payments on your credit cards might not be in your interest

Strangely enough, you're more likely to be sued for medical bills than credit card debts. The reason relates to the statute of limitations. You'll recall from previous discussions that the statute of limitations on credit card debt is six years, and it starts at the time of your last payment, not when the debt was incurred. Thus, if the credit card company can get you to make a payment, then it can keep moving the statute of limitations forward. If you're not going to pay a credit card debt, then you shouldn't make any more payments at all on that account. Once you do, you reset the statute of limitations and give the collector more time to sue you for the debt. Credit card companies are very aware of this, and the strategy when they contact you is usually to convince you to make small payments so as to reset the statute of limitations.

14. What You Need to Know about the Law Office of Patrick McBurney

Since July 29, 1995, the Law Office of Patrick McBurney has been a full-service law firm headquartered in the Tri-Cities of Washington State. Its primary mission is to provide competent and affordable legal representation to debtors in Chapter 7 and Chapter 13 bankruptcy cases. That mission includes serving the entire State of Washington by expanding to locations in Spokane, Vancouver, and Seattle.

14.1. Who is Patrick McBurney?

My name is Patrick McBurney, and I own and operate the McBurney Law Office. I've been an attorney for over a quarter of a century. Although born in California, I've been a resident of Washington since the age of eleven. I've practiced law in Idaho, Washington, and am also admitted to the Bar of North Dakota, as well as the Federal Bar Association for the Western and Eastern Districts of Washington. I'm a member of the National Association of Chapter Thirteen Trustee's Organization (NACTT) and am a member of the National Association of Consumer Bankruptcy Attorneys (NACBA). I've represented thousands of clients as a bankruptcy attorney, public defender, criminal defense attorney, and family law attorney. I've managed a whole range of complex legal cases such as bankruptcy litigation as well as contract disputes, DUIs, criminal misdemeanors, criminal felonies, divorces, probates, and child support issues. I'm also a certified mediator.

While I've had a diverse practice over many years, the area I enjoy working in the most is bankruptcy. It's one of the most intellectually-challenging areas of the law. Moreover, of all the areas of law I have experience in, bankruptcy is the one in which I think I'm able to help my clients the most. I can do a very good job in a divorce case, but I find that my clients are almost always worse off than when the case started. I can do good work in a criminal case, but my client may still go to jail (perhaps for a lot less time, but to jail nonetheless). Bankruptcy is the one area of practice in which my clients are almost always better off at the end of the case than they were at the beginning.

This is why I've dedicated myself to the practice of bankruptcy law, and why after over 25 years, I've become exceptionally good at it. I've learned that if you want to make a difference, then it's a matter of helping one client at a time—one person at a time. When I do a bankruptcy case, I make a difference in someone's life by relieving them of the stress and anxiety they feel in the middle of a financial storm.

14.2. How can the Law office of Patrick McBurney help you with your financial problem?

When you have a financial problem, when you're overwhelmed with debt, when you're being harassed and sued by creditors, you can easily lose your sense of direction. A good lawyer can help you draw a map out of the financial storm. At the law office of Patrick McBurney:

1. We offer flexible appointments: The office is open weekdays from 9:00 a.m. to 5:00 p.m. If we can't meet during normal business hours, I'm very willing to work with you to find a time that fits your schedule. I can often meet clients after hours or on Saturday, for example.

2. We offer flat rates for legal services: Most lawyers bill you on an hourly basis. You don't want to pay a lawyer every time he answers the phone or thinks about your case. You want certainty about how much your case will cost. You need an attorney who is an expert you can afford. This is why I charge flat rates for bankruptcy.

3. We offer payment flexibility and payment plans. I have good news and bad news on this. First, the bad news—before I can file your Chapter 7 bankruptcy case, I need to be paid in full. Now, the good news—for a nominal retainer, I'll start representation and take payments until the fee is paid and the case can be filed. In a Chapter 13 case, I can start at a lower cost of entry and get paid through the Chapter 13 plan (remember, though, that Chapter 13 takes between three to five years and is more expensive than Chapter 7).

4. We provide expert legal services for bankruptcy: In over 25 years, I've represented more than 2,000 people in bankruptcy matters all over Washington State. It's no exaggeration to say that I'm one of the best consumer bankruptcy lawyers in Washington. I

went to law school because I wanted to make a difference. Over the years, I've come to realize more and
more that every client I meet offers me an opportunity
to make that difference. I'm looking forward to the
opportunity to help you with your financial storm.

14.3. How can I get a free consultation?

I charge a consultation fee. The only things I have to sell
are my time and my expert advice. Normally, I charge up to
$150.00 for a thirty-minute consultation. In this book, I've
attempted to answer the most common questions about
bankruptcy. If you've read my book and want a consultation,
most likely you need to hire a bankruptcy lawyer. In that
case, when you contact my office to make your appointment,
simply tell us that you've "read the book," and I'll gladly
waive the consultation fee.

Thank you for having read this book. I hope you found
the advice useful. Feel free to reach out by calling 509-374-
8996 or emailing at www.patrickmcburney.com.

www.ingramcontent.com/pod-product-compliance
Lightning Source LLC
Chambersburg PA
CBHW070409200326
41518CB00011B/2122